Forks in the Road

Tom Leslie:
Your impact on
this profession and
society is enormous.
May it be even
greater.

Also By RICHARD WEINGARDT

Seeing Into The Future: The I Book (Editor)

Sound the Charge

Engineering Colorado (with Fu Hau Chen)

Cylindrical Shell Design

WHAT INDUSTRY LEADERS SAY ABOUT
FORKS IN THE ROAD:

"A passionate cheerleader and a caring critic, Rich Weingardt shares his keen insights on engineers and engineering—his frustration, his admiration, and his unshakable confidence in engineers' ability to get the job done. 'The world is run by those who show up,' this dynamic engineering leader says. But getting to the right place isn't easy; forks punctuate the road. Which way to turn? This insightful, spirited work makes it clear."

> — JOHN P. BACHNER, Executive Director, ASFE
> President, Bachner Communications

"With Forks in the Road, *Weingardt has sounded a clarion call for engineers who seek to influence our increasingly complex and dynamic world. His prophetic message is clear; today's engineer must become tomorrow's leader—for the sake of us all."*

> — GEORGE BLANKS, Director, Engineering Leadership
> Institute, Auburn University

"Weingardt has provided a recipe for engineers to improve their lot in life. He practices what he preaches and continually encourages us to 'show up.' He influences through leadership drawing on his many years in the front lines."

> — R. WAYNE BOWES, Vice President, FIDIC
> Vice President, DELCAN Canada

"This book, presented in distinct separately readable chapters, is a must for engineers who wish to be leaders in society while being successful engineers. The author has done a superb job of writing: the book uses the English language in an easily read style that effectively communicates. Both engineers and non-engineers should find the book both informative and interesting."

> — A. RAY CHAMBERLAIN, Former President, Colorado
> State University; Former Director, Colorado Department
> of Transportation

Continued

"This wide-ranging collection of essays is a readable, often intriguing, mixture of memoir and message. As the founder of an international consulting engineering firm, Weingardt chronicles the path which he took to success, including some of his personal forks in the road and his philosophy of doing business. However, the more compelling message which recurs in several of the chapters is that twenty-first-century engineers must not be content with their twentieth-century image and behavior.

"They must evolve from relatively obscure solvers of problems, becoming highly visible influencers of important societal decisions and, hence, shapers of the future trends. To this end, Weingardt offers ample justification for this role change. He presents suggestions and role models to help present and future engineers navigate this critical fork in the road. In a world dominated by technology, engineers must not just do things right, but help assure that society works on the right things."

> — DAVID R. CLAIR, Former President, Exxon Research and Engrg.; Executive Vice President (Ret.), Exxon International

"Forks in the Road is Richard Weingardt's passionate vision for the engineering (and design) profession for the coming years. He calls it as he sees it, names names, gives colorful examples from the accomplishments of others, and offers his own insightful keys for success."

> — RICHARD CROWELL, Senior Vice President, DPIC Companies, Inc.

"In Forks in the Road, Richard Weingardt brings a seasoned practitioner's knowledge and experience to many of the issues confronting the consulting engineer's profession. Combining an informal style with personal history and anecdote, he describes his vision of the 'Complete Engineer'."

> — ALBERT A. DORMAN, Chairman, DMJM Founding Chairman, AECOM Technology Corporation

"With engaging gusto and contagious enthusiasm, Richard Weingardt calls upon his fellow engineers to 'show up,' become involved, and take leadership responsibilities. He argues persuasively that this is the way for individual engineers to achieve their goals, and for the profession as a whole to achieve appropriate recognition of its good works."

> — SAMUEL C. FLORMAN, Author, *The Civilized Engineer*
> Partner, Kreisler, Borg, Florman

"Richard Weingardt is a leader among structural engineering consultants, and is uniquely qualified to write a book on the need for engineers to recognize their importance as wealth creators and leaders in society. The book is unusually readable and interesting. Weingardt has been able to weave his varied experiences as a very successful consulting engineer for 32 years into sound lessons for the engineering profession. He provides some excellent ideas on improving the education of engineers to ensure that they have the background to be professionals.

"His chapter on '10 Commandments of Marketing' should be read by every engineer. He has proven that they are essential to the growth and success of a company.

"I really liked the chapters on improving the image of engineers and the need for engineers to be involved in leadership positions. I am going to make certain that my freshman engineering class is aware of the principles he presents.

"Weingardt has a great chapter on women entrepreneurs. I wish my daughters could have read this when they were considering their future careers.

"His chapter on 'Partnering with Gorillas' should be read by every architect and engineer. Teamwork in the design and construction process is the vital key to faster completions, lower costs and happier owners.

"The chapters on 'Tomorrow's Engineer' and 'Seeing Into The Future' should be required reading for every engineering graduate. There is a wealth of practical, insightful information."

> — DAVID W. FOWLER, Taylor Professor in Engrg., Univ. of Texas; Director, International Ctr. for Aggregates Research
> *Continued*

"Drawing on his vast experience in the public and private sectors reinforced with extensive research, Rich Weingardt's Forks in the Road *bravely points the way for a new and more socially relevant engineer—one not only technically competent, but INVOLVED.*

"Whether electing a technical or management track (fork), Weingardt forcefully argues that all must be involved in the broader community.

"Loaded with practical advice on the science, business, and art of engineering, the author is convincing in explaining why engineers must be leaders, not only contributors and participants. He is helpfully specific on 'how.'

"The engineering profession needs a futurist like Weingardt who sees beyond the end of the project toward an exciting role for engineers in a better, sustainable future."

— GENERAL (Ret.) HANK HATCH, Former Head of U.S. Army Corps of Engrs.; President, Fluor Daniel-Hanford

"A roadmap for members of the 'invisible profession' written by a respected practitioner who leads by example."

— J.M. STEYN LAUBSCHER, President, International Federation of Consulting Engineers (FIDIC)

"Richard Weingardt brings his lifelong experiences as both a worker and manager as insight to the engineering world of the future. His thoughts and perceptions are well worth reading."

— JAMES McANALLY, President (Ret.), Lockheed Martin Astronautics

"Forks in the Road is truly a 'Wake up Call' — a call to action for the engineering community. Weingardt not only identifies a myriad of problems and self-inflicted wounds, but also provides a blueprint and plan for action for engineers to follow. This is a 'must read' book for those who want to take the steps required to help engineers regain their rightful leadership roles in our industry."

— HENRY L. MICHEL, Chairman Emeritus, Parsons Brinckerhoff, Inc.

"Mr. Weingardt has thrown down the gauntlet. Engineers must take a leadership role, not an advisory role in the proper use and development of technology. His book challenges all engineers, but in particular beginning engineers, to prepare themselves for this expanded role in society."

For any of us to obtain leadership (as opposed to advisory) roles in society, we must first become leaders in the field of engineering. This means obtaining a solid knowledge of fundamental engineering principles, committing yourself to lifetime learning, and having a strong desire to assume leadership roles in our professional societies. Mr. Weingardt, in his book, provides numerous examples of how this can be accomplished. The second step for engineers to take involves demonstrating our value to society in a technological world. Decisions are constantly being made by those who have no scientific or engineering backgrounds.

"Engineers need to become more visible so that ordinary citizens in our society desire, or even demand, that technology decisions come primarily from engineers. This is also addressed by Mr. Weingardt and he offers many examples as to how this can be achieved by the engineering profession. It is time for engineers to redirect their effort and energy in order to assume responsibility for society's future - not to leave our society's destiny in the hands of those academics, bureaucrats, politicians and others who lack technical expertise."

> — WALTER P. MOORE, Thomas Bulloch Chair & Professor at Texas A&M; Chairman, Walter P. Moore & Associates

"Richard Weingardt's passion for engineering is contagious. His book combines many years of successful engineering practice with some important notions and stimulating ideas on engineers as leaders. For those with the desire to lead, he offers challenges and thoughts on how to make it happen."

> — M.A. MORTENSON, JR., Chairman and CEO, Mortenson Construction

Continued

"As it suggests, this book goes in several directions at the same time; it is part folksy wisdom and part shrewd business practice, part autobiography and part inspirational eloquence. Only Richard Weingardt could have written this call to engineers to take up the challenge of leadership in society."

— ANTHANASIOS MOULAKIS, Herbst Professor of Humanities for Engineers, University of Colo at Boulder

"Forks in the Road is must reading for leaders and engineers. Rich Weingardt puts into perspective the reality of technology in today's world in an insightful and humorous manner. He stresses the need for engineers to become actively involved. As he suggests, engineers should take their ability to solve problems and put it to work in their communities to make this a better world for future generations."

— THOMAS E. NORTON, President of Colorado Senate 1998 Gubernatorial Candidate-Colorado

"Richard Weingardt's call to the American engineer 'to spring to action' and exert leadership is also a very opportune message for the engineering community worldwide. As we move on to global engineering, it is even more urgent to use our creativity to identify and implement the paradigm shift our profession needs for the new millennium."

— FELIPE OCHOA, 1995 & 1996 President, CNEC Mexico Member, Executive Committee, FIDIC

"Forks in the Road makes it immensely clear there is a need for engineering to be advanced to a professional level. Because of the four-year course load of the engineer and the explosion of technological advances, one cannot adequately learn the numerous areas of impact the engineer has on society. Weingardt clearly makes the case that additional education, particularly in the humanities and social studies, is necessary for tomorrow's engineers."

— C.R. "CHUCK" PENNONI, President, ABET; Past Pres., ASCE; Interim President of Drexel University 1994/95

"Weingardt's Forks in the Road *is not only an interesting collection of succinct case studies about the excitement and challenges of the engineering profession, but a detailed guide on the ingredients to become successful. He challenges each engineer to take the risks of leadership in society's policy decisions and to help redirect engineering education to include leadership skills in the broad world within which engineers work. Weingardt describes the electronic age of engineering and the global opportunities available to U.S. engineers.*

"It is refreshing to read about the value of bridges to society, the successful careers of women consulting engineers and what the profession can become if we 'just go do it.' This is a reference manual for all members of the project team—the owner, the architect, the numerous engineering specialists, the contractors and all stakeholders in the constructed project. It is rare to find such a broad but vital array of non-technical issues addressed in one publication. These issues, when taken together can redirect the future of the engineering profession."

> — JAMES W. POIROT, Former Chairman, CH2M Hill
> Past President, ASCE; Vice President, World Federation
> of Engineering Organizations

"The author has taken up the challenge of addressing the problems that beset the engineering profession, and promoting the actions engineers must take if their true contributions to society are to be recognized. I know of no one who undertakes this task so energetically or persuasively as Weingardt. He is indeed a champion of the profession."

> — ROBERT D. REITH, Past President, European Federation
> of Engrg. Consult. Assoc; Past Chairman, Association of
> Consulting Engineers U.K.

"A most timely publication. Mr. Weingardt alerts readers to the importance of improving engineers' image—imperative if the U.S. is to maintain its economic and technological edge in the 21st century."

> — JILL S. TIETJEN, Past President, Society of Women
> Engineers

Forks in the Road

Impacting The World Around Us

Richard Weingardt

PALAMAR
Publishing

Denver, Colorado

Forks In The Road by Richard Weingardt
is available at a discount when ordered in bulk quantities.
For information, contact **Palamar Publishing,**
a division of Jacqueline Enterprises, Inc.
3010 South Garfield Street, Denver, CO 80210

Design by David R. Weingardt

ISBN: 0-932446-05-1 (Perfect Bound)
ISBN: 0-932446-07-8 (Hard Back)

Library of Congress Cataloging in Publication Data
Weingardt, Richard G.
Forks in the Road. Includes Index.
1. Engineering. 2. Leadership. 3. Management. 4. Business.
5. Education. 6. Community Involvement. 7. Politics. 8. Title

Library of Congress Catalog 97-076151

PRINTED IN THE UNITED STATES OF AMERICA

10 9 8 7 6 5 4 3 2 1

To my parents, Martin and Caroline,

and to all

those who go that extra mile to make the world a better place.

ACKNOWLEDGMENTS

I am much indebted to Jeff Rundles, long-time friend and confidant, for his continued support and encouragement to put into writing my lifetime philosophies about engineering (engineering life and the bigger picture), and for being a most wise and critical sounding board. His advice during the evolution of many of the ideas in this book, as well as his assistance with editing and improving the author's writing style, was invaluable. My thanks go to Barbara McNichol for an outstanding job of copy-editing and to Michele Ashmore for final proofing.

In the front of the book is a list of engineering and industry leaders — giants in this profession — with their thoughts about *Forks In The Road*. I am very thankful to them for reading the final draft of my manuscript, and most appreciative of them sharing their thoughts about it.

There are many others — too many to mention — friends, associates and colleagues — who have offered encouragement over the years and deserve appreciation. Their suggestions, comments and thoughts constructively helped give perspective to many of my ideas. So without naming you individually, I say thank you to each and every one of you.

Finally, I thank my family to whom I am deeply grateful for their support and encouragement, and for always being there when I needed that extra little boost. I am most beholden to my dear wife of 38 years, Evelyn, who has been such a major force in my life and career. She has stuck it out with me through all the good times, and all the bad times. Without her support, and that of my son, David, and all the others referred to above, this book would not have been possible.

FOREWORD

What better testimony to the significance of engineering than the tribute offered by U.S. President Herbert Hoover in the early 1950s:

"It is a great profession. There is the fascination of watching a figment of imagination emerge through the aid of science to a plan on paper. Then it moves to realization in stone or metal or energy. Then it brings jobs and homes to men. Then it elevates the standard of living and adds to the comforts of life. That is the engineer's high privilege.

"The great liability of the engineer compared to men of other professions is that his works are out in the open where all can see them. His acts, step by step, are in hard substance. He cannot bury his mistakes in the grave like doctors. He cannot argue them into thin air or blame the judge like lawyers. He cannot, like the architects, cover his failures with trees and vines. He cannot, like the politicians, screen his shortcomings by blaming his opponents and hope that people forget. The engineer simply cannot deny he did it. If his works do not work, he is damned.

"On the other hand, unlike the doctor, his is not a life among the weak. Unlike the soldier, destruction is not his purpose. Unlike the lawyer, quarrels are not his daily bread. To the engineer falls the job of clothing the bare bones of science with life, comfort and hope. No doubt as the years go by people forget which engineer did it, even if they ever knew. Or some politician puts his name on it. Or they credit it to some promoter who used other people's money. But the engineer himself looks back at the unending stream of goodness which flows from his successes with satisfactions that few professions may know. And the verdict of his fellow professional is all the accolade he wants." (From: Hoover, Herbert, *Addresses Upon the American Road,* Stanford University Press, 1955.)

I have always been inspired by these passages*, and I have always strived to live up to the ideals Hoover expressed. This book, among other things, takes Hoover one better, however. It calls on engineers, both men and women, to be leaders outside the immediacy of their professional work, to lead and to contribute to society through public debate and community involvement. Leadership is its own reward, and the benefits of encouraging more leadership by engineers, I truly believe, will help ensure that the future is secure.

(*Footnote: In reflecting on Hoover's message, it is judicious to keep in mind that, in his day, nearly all engineers were men, and the downplaying of other professions was not "politically incorrect" — hence his wording and analogies.)

CONTENTS

INTRODUCTION

"When you come to a fork in the road — take it!"
—Yogi Berra

Engineers make things run, but engineers rarely run things. With more than 10 million engineers worldwide (2.5 million in the U.S.) there is awesome potential for power and influence in setting public policy and direction. Engineers are probably the single most indispensable group needed for maintaining and expanding the world's economic well-being and its standard of living. Yet few from this group are in the forefront of leadership in society.

Much of this is because of the very nature of those who select engineering as a career, and how they are educated and trained. Engineers tend to be content with — and receive tremendous satisfaction from — just solving the problem. Their reward, as underscored by President Hoover's portrait of an engineer, is the satisfaction of their work and the good their solutions will bring.

Public recognition, fame and fortune are not what drive them. This is part of the problem. Though laudable, these traits create a roadblock that must be navigated around for engineers to lead and make the world a better place for future generations. Modern society is much too dependent on technology for its guidance to have a void of technical leadership — those who can do the work.

The world is run by those who show up, and the need for more and more engineers to show up in "big picture" policy and decision-making positions is more critical now than ever before. This book is a collection of reflections, essays and practical advice on how this can be accomplished, and why engineers should become involved in leadership in their communities and society. It is targeted to the thinking engineer, either someone currently working in industry or the newly graduated engineer with visions of doing more to impact the world around us — someone not content to just be in the background computing "nuts and bolts" or accepting the "nerd" image.

Each chapter is a stand-alone essay which can be read in any order. Through example and encouragement, the book offers a variety of strategies for taking charge. It presents engineers with paths to follow in their careers to bring more meaning to what they do and show how they fit into the broader community. Many of the book's insights and recommendations will appeal to individuals in other technical professions, as well: those who solve problems and contribute in a meaningful way to everyone's standard of life — architects, doctors, accountants, geologists, inventors, construction managers, etc.

When you look at life's landscape and the adventures it holds for each of us, it is amazing how many experiences transcend professions, and how taking different forks in the road in one are the same for all career paths. We all struggle with which is the right way to go as we seek our place in history. Which forks do we take? Remember the part in *Alice in Wonderland* where she asks the Cheshire Cat which way to go? When the Cat replies, "That depends a good deal on where you want to get to." Alice says, "I don't much care where." The Cat then comments, "Then it doesn't matter which way you walk." When she adds that she doesn't care "so long as I get somewhere," the Cat says, "Oh, you're sure to do that, if only you walk long enough!" (From: Carroll, Lewis: *Alice in Wonderland*.)

Hopefully, this book will give you food for thought about (and a better sense of purpose on) where you want to go, how you want to get there, and how long you want to take doing it. And I hope it will inflame your passion to be the "best there ever was" in the profession of your choice.

My experience for the last 38 years has been as a design engineer, first with a federal agency, then with a well-established consulting engineering firm and finally as the owner of my own company, Richard Weingardt Consultants, Inc. Heading my own firm means "the buck stops here" and it brings plenty of headaches. But the rewards are exhilarating. I've had many wonderful, exciting and successful experiences — major designs completed in nearly every state and in more than a dozen foreign countries — that form the basis of my current philosophy about the profession of engineering and engineers.

I grew up in a construction family — my father was a general contractor — and I always wanted to build things or be involved in getting them built. My father was a hard-working German, a first-generation American, with integrity and a strong sense of right and wrong. From him I learned many things, not the least of which was that a person's reputation is sacred. He also taught me that enjoying the journey, as well as the fulfillment of the goal, is part of life too.

Throughout my career, I have been seriously involved with both engineering associations and community affairs. I have often pondered the lack of widespread commitment to these pursuits by my fellow engineers. I am dismayed that only ten percent of those who graduate with engineering degrees ever become registered professional engineers (P.E.s). This book reflects on these concerns.

Several of the book's essays have appeared in some form or the other in various publications. They include various journals of the American Society of Civil Engineers, *American*

Consulting Engineer, The Bent, Beratende Ingenieure, Civil Engineering News, Colorado Business Magazine, The Daily Journal, The Denver Business Journal, The Denver Post, Engineering Times, and *Engineering News Record.*

Forks In The Road challenges engineers to get involved in both their industry and in society — to become citizens of the world. It encourages us to be the best in our field — world-class leaders as well as leading-edge technical experts — so we can better impact what goes on around us. Its intent is to open our eyes to the possibilities available in this profession so we can take the best forks in the road throughout our careers.

1

ROAD FORKS

"Coming together is a beginning; keeping together is progress; working together is success."

—Henry Ford

It was a relatively small sphere — only the size of an average pumpkin, weighing less than 190 pounds — yet it astonished the world, shocked Americans and changed the course of modern history. Overnight the feat, hurling Sputnik into orbit, focused attention on science and engineering, and elevated the status of both. Up until that fateful day in October of 1957, a complacency and false sense of security reigned in this country. Now there was panic — a panic that the technical achievements of the Soviet's engineers had moved them ahead of us as leaders in space exploration. We were in the "cold war" and the military implications were foreboding.

Indeed, doubts were raised about the status of U.S. engineering and technological industries in general. The nation suddenly became aware of the impact engineering had (and would have) on its way of life. There was a general call for more science and technology education, and the government stepped up the development of the American space program.

As a result, many young people became fascinated with space, rockets and astronauts, and many became infatuated with the idea of becoming an engineer.

In 1961, President John F. Kennedy, the first U.S. president born in the 20th century, challenged the nation to do more for public service. ("Ask not what your country can do for you. Ask what you can do for your country.") He invented the "peace corps" and made a commitment to put an American on the moon before the decade was out. This became a stunning challenge to the country and its engineering and technological communities, and it was answered. Enrollments in engineering colleges skyrocketed.

The engineered products and systems, now in everyday use, that resulted from Kennedy's space challenge are far too vast to count (some say more than 100,000 usable devices) — the heart pacemaker, satellites, laser controls, guidance systems, etc.

The U.S. space program is but one of the many engineering-intensive periods throughout history that have vaulted society (and its quality of life) forward in monumental leaps. It exemplifies how closely interwoven are engineering and civilization and, according to Wernher Von Braun, renowned engineer and rocket scientist, even the meaning of life. To paraphrase Von Braun: "The more comfortable we get with space (and space exploration), the more we understand about the universe, and the more we understand ourselves and what life is all about."

When enough time has passed and the epic history books are written, the man-to-the-moon saga will surely rank as one of the greatest periods in recorded history — a time of major engineering achievement and the precursor to the era we are now in. Today, engineering is too inter-related with everything in the world around us for engineers to be narrowly focused, concerned only about technical issues.

To better grasp how we got to where we are and the inter-action between engineering and the progress of humankind, it is useful to take a look back through history. Several chroni-clers have laid out the different eras of engineering. I like the following two the best. I have found them different enough that, by combining them, one can come up with a sound per-spective on the engineers' impact on the world. What will be illustrated is: *The history of engineering is, in many ways, the his-tory of the human race itself.*

THE AGES OF ENGINEERING

In his "Plenary Session Address" at the University of Col-orado's 1993 Centennial Symposium of the College of Engi-neering (which the author moderated), Norman Augustine, former CEO of Lockheed-Martin, the giant aerospace compa-ny, suggested the history of engineering could be divided into five distinct engineering ages: Structural, Mechanical, Electri-cal, Information and Socio-Engineering. Each of these ages has a beginning but no end, and we have basically been through the first four. We are now in the throes of the fifth age. Just as with civilization itself, each age of engineering builds on its past.

The "Structural Age" (starting around 3000 B.C.) reflects the human race's ongoing challenge to construct shelters and other physical structures that did not (and do not) fall down. Gravity was (and is) engineering's principal enemy.

From the mid-1700s, we had what is generally known as the Industrial Revolution or the "Mechanical Age of Engineer-ing." During this period, the principles of engineering were applied to designing and building mechanical devices. The common enemy was friction. According to Augustine, "The ultimate examples of the Mechanical Age included the steamship, the railroad engine, the automobile and the airplane."

"The one exhibit that overshadowed even the mighty Ferris Wheel (the 265-foot high feature attraction) at the World Exposition in 1893 (in Chicago) was the Electricity Building, which demonstrated this new phenomenon and its ability to power devices that provided mechanical force, heat, light and communications," stated Augustine. It was part of what he identified as the "Electrical Age of Engineering," which started in the late 1870s. During this period were built, great dams to generate electricity and complex power systems to distribute it. Engineers designed sophisticated appliances and devices to make use of it as well.

How significant electricity has become can be demonstrated by using the airplane as an example. Augustine points out that "about one-tenth of one percent of an aircraft's weight in the 1920s was devoted to electrical devices. By the 1940s, this had increased to fully one percent. In the 1980s, in the case of military fighter airplanes, it had become 10 percent of the airplane's weight — and one-third of its cost."

The fourth engineering age proposed is the "Information Age," which started in 1906 when Lee De Forest invented the vacuum tube. "From the vacuum tube to the transistor to the integrated circuit, these devices enhanced the human mind in the same way that the Mechanical Age magnified humankind's muscles," Augustine said. During this time, engineers freed people "of routine mental pursuits" and vastly extended "their capacity." In contrast to preceding times, what was moved, altered and manipulated was knowledge and not things.

Augustine's fifth age, which starts in 1979, he calls "The Socio-Engineering Age." He said, "Today, we take for granted that telephones work, skyscrapers don't fall down, airline travel is boringly safe, automobiles start, electric lights go on when you flip on the switch, computers do not make errors, and televisions not only bring you more than 100 channels of programming but do so in virtually perfect color. But despite the many positive contributions of our profession, and despite all the amazing technological innovations that are constantly being produced, many of the greatest challenges for engineers today come from non-engineering sources."

Significant in this "Socio-Engineering Age," he stated, is that engineers of tomorrow must recognize that we "are no longer constrained simply by the laws of nature as was generally the case in the past" but we must "become as adept with dealing with societal and political forces as with gravitational and electromagnetic forces."

Many times technology and engineering are perceived as the problem rather than the solution. Often times, he said, "The word 'technology' conjures up images of Chernobyl, Bhopal, Thalidomide, the Exxon Valdez, Challenger and atomic bombs." Much of the public's discomfort with the use of new technology can be tied to these types of "failures" and events like the Three-Mile Island nuclear power plant incident in 1987. They have a significant impact on the public's willingness to accept, on faith, every new innovation that engineers come up with.

To continue to generate technological progress that will enhance the lives of everyone, as we move into the next millennium, engineers need to combine the strengths of engineering with the far broader skills needed to prosper in the 21st century. These skills include stronger interpersonal skills and more in-depth knowledge of politics, economics, history and geography. Engineers, having such broadened skills, will be invaluable at the highest levels of leadership in society, to deal effectively with the huge range of issues confronting a world increasingly dependent on technology.

Many deep thinkers like Isaac Asimov (author of *The Intelligent Man's Guide to Science*) remind us that more and more "our leaders must deal with dangers that threaten the entire world, where an understanding of those dangers and the possible solutions depend on a good grasp of science." He suggests that issues, for instance, like the greenhouse effect, acid rain and pollution, and even questions on diet, "require scientific literacy."

CATALYSTS FOR PROGRESS

The perspective on the effect of engineering throughout history, by using the aforementioned five ages of engineering, causes different reflection than the more traditional breakdown of eras such as those in Darling, Kilgour, Kirby and Withington's (DKKW) *Engineering in History*. They break the major impacts of engineering into the following divisions: Urban Society, Greek Engineering, Roman Engineering, The Revolution of Power, Foundations for Industry, The Industrial Revolution, Roads-Canals-Bridges, Steam Vessels and Locomotives, Iron and Steel, Electrical Engineering, Modern Transportation, and Sanitary and Hydraulic Engineering. The text, written in 1956, mostly predates computers, rockets, nuclear power and the information technologies.

In the "Urban Society" era, the engineer dealt with housing and shelter, and irrigation. Its roots go far back in human history. Egyptian engineering controlled the Nile River and built the great pyramids. The Egyptians so marveled at the works of Imhotep, the engineer and builder of the first great pyramid Saqqura, that after he died they put him in the awesome company of their gods, and worshiped him as one. It's been a long time since engineers were treated like that! The Greeks created the Acropolis, and the Roman engineers, among other great works, produced durable roads, aqueducts and water supplies. These societies gave the world the so-called Seven Wonders of The World, what we now refer to as the Wonders of Antiquity. They were all marvels made possible by engineers and engineering.

"Water, wind, and animal power were the major sources of nonhuman power which medieval engineers developed. The new prime movers were used to operate many types of machines invented during the Middle Ages," state DKKW in describing the "Revolution of Power" era. The "foundations for industry" engineers included the likes of Leonardo da Vinci, by far the most famous engineer of the 17th century. Engineers of this period greatly advanced the use of mathematics and scientific principles in the design of buildings, bridges, canals and harbors, and for municipal engineering. They increased the use of water and fire for power, and readied the world for the Industrial Revolution. The rest, as they say, is history.

The modern civilization and living standard we enjoy today has largely been made possible because of the many contributions of engineers throughout the ages. If no engineering minds ever existed, we would still travel at horse-speed, carry water by buckets, talk long distance by yelling, live in and work in unlighted spaces without air-conditioning or central heat, and be without radios, televisions and computers. Without engineers, there would be no high-rise buildings, long-span bridges, interstate highway or rail systems, water-control dams, nor tunnels under mountains or waterways. There would be no high-speed aircraft, trains, automobiles, boats nor sophisticated medical devices; no laser-control systems, orbiting satellites nor the Internet. And man would never have walked on the moon. More people today would be dying young from contaminated water, spoiled food, and unsanitary conditions than of old age, or cancer or heart disease.

NOT EVERYTHING HAS BEEN INVENTED

The magnificent impact of engineering, however, is but in its infancy. When one reflects on how far we have advanced in such a short span of time, and how well the modern world functions, it is easy to get fooled into thinking most of what can be done has been done. It reminds me of two classic underestimations: one by the 1899 head of the U.S. Patent Office, Charles Duell, who urged President McKinley to abolish the place because "Everything that can be invented has been invented." The other was by a senior IBM engineer, commenting in 1968 on the then-new microchip: "But what....is it good for?"

There is much left to do to enhance humankind's standards — much that only engineers are trained, equipped and educated to do. There are an infinite number of new products to create and systems to design and build. We are only beginning to really harness nature and explore space. In addition to creating new products and systems, engineers are needed to solve the daily problems of repairing what has been built in the past. They are also needed to design, build and maintain new infrastructure for both the present and future generations.

The world's population is approaching nine billion. One-third of the world's people live in poverty, and many of the earth's rivers and lakes, not to mention portions of the seas, are polluted or fully contaminated. Engineers and scientists urgently need to devise solutions for the plight facing us concerning environmental issues: the greenhouse effect, the hole in the ozone layer, polluted air and water, contaminated soils, and hazardous waste problems, as well as the basic management of staggering amounts of all types of man-made waste.

Engineers have done more (and will continue to do more) than any other single group to protect the environment and this earth. The necessity to elevate the world's awareness to our infrastructure needs and environmental problems is quietly but quickly creeping up on us. The need for a sound international policy on "sustainable development" is one of the first steps.

We desperately need engineers who are trained to solve problems to maintain our eroding, wealth-creating potential and help expand the world's economic pie. The list of issues engineers can and will be called on to solve is endless.

Since there will always be a tremendous need for creative engineers, there is no authentic fear we will be replaced by computers. Rather, we will be their masters. I have a real concern, however, and that is: Unless we reassess our role in society — rethink the value of our contributions and how we fit into the bigger picture of things — society will continue to relegate us to the role of technician and not professional.

OUR GREATEST STRENGTH

One of our greatest strengths is also our major weakness: the satisfaction we derive from our work, our accomplishments. We do not need the limelight to be satisfied. If we feel we have given it our all — if we are pleased with what we have done — we are content. As President Hoover pointed out, "the verdict" of our "fellow professional is all the accolade" we want. Because of this — as well as the fact that many who choose this line of work tend to be introverts — we and our accomplishments are often overlooked, unless something falls down or does not work — or a Sputnik hits the scene.

At this stage, several forks in the road can be pursued. The profession of engineering — indeed, the world at large — has reached a fork in the road, and it is time for engineers to take action.

The first step is for more and more of us to get out of our

shells and join the public debate, become community leaders influencing public policy and direction. This world is too dependent on engineering to leave it totally in the hands of those who are technically illiterate. As many engineers as possible must take on leadership roles, not just in this industry, but in our communities and in society — at the table where far-reaching decisions are made. We must become advocates for the wise investment in infrastructure and plans needed to deal with our environmental problems. We must determine how we can sustain development on this planet so future generations will not suffer.

CHANGES ARE NEEDED

To position ourselves to accomplish these things, two significant changes have to occur within the engineering ranks. First, we need to broaden our perspective and become citizens of the world. Second, we need to become more visible and outspoken about engineering and its impact on our communities. Both these topics are covered in more detail in following chapters.

If we are to be effective in either of the above, we need to hone our communications and people skills — and our natural leadership skills. And, very importantly, something has to be changed about how engineers are educated. We, who have long since walked the halls in the ivy-covered buildings of higher education, will have to do with what education and inspiration we got in our days, and become the mentors (and the role models) for those coming after us. We have to get involved now, as leaders in society, so we can leave a great legacy to the next generations of engineers who can be even greater than we were (or are).

Samuel Florman, author of *The Introspective Engineer* and *The Civilized Engineer*, says, "It is important that engineers — or at least a goodly number of them — come forward to play a prominent role in American society." To do this, he feels engineers must be smart and broadly educated. He adds: "It is also important that engineers become more effective in a technical sense as well: creative and competent, able to keep the U.S. in the forefront of the industrial world."

NEW WAYS TO EDUCATE ENGINEERS

Breaking tradition to change how we educate and train engineers will help make them more effective and bring them into the center of civic activity. Through education, we must arouse in our future engineers (and practicing ones as well) both a passion for the profession, and a commitment to life-long learning that will last long after college graduation.

What has always struck me about my engineering education, beyond how narrowly focused it was, is how isolated we engineers seemed to be — how what we do did not seem to relate to the "outside world." We were bright and part of an exclusive club: people who knew how to deal with facts and scientific principles. And boy, could we solve problems where such knowledge was necessary. But it was never ingrained in me until much later in my career what an important part of life and civilization engineers and their work was (and is).

I do not remember a single professor (and I had several excellent ones) who stood before us and pontificated on what a grand and noble profession we were about to embark upon — on the impact our work would have on society. Very few instilled in us how engineering meshed into the world around us or challenged us to go forth and become active participants in our communities.

Stuart Walesh, author of *Engineering Your Future*, states that "the root cause" of the "lack of leadership" problems we engineers face is "the way we educate engineers." He adds, "If the engineering profession does not create a new education paradigm, others will create it for us. The others will be attorneys, developers, financiers, businesspersons and legislators. They will continue to expand their roles as deciders and directors in the infrastructure and environmental arena while we engineers will, by default, be relegated even more to the 'doer' function. Unless we change our engineering education paradigm, engineers will be even more 'on tap' and less 'on top'."

Because of the tremendous course load just to get all the technical education necessary to be a good engineer — along with a sprinkling of non-technical subjects — it takes the average engineering student more than four-and-a-half years to get a four-year bachelor's degree. And they still end up getting short-changed on the humanities and liberal arts classes — classes needed to fill out a person's education and make him or her well rounded, ready for leadership.

Walter Moore, Jr., professor of the endowed Thomas Bullock Chair for Leadership and Innovation at Texas A&M, is convinced leadership awareness is an ingrained part of his institution's consciousness, maybe because of its past military traditions. As believed by Moore: "A&M was founded, not to just educate engineers, but to turn out leaders. That spirit seeps through into everything. Our students are immersed in outside activities: church groups, engineering societies and the community." He also reported, "In my classes, part of a student's grade is dependent on his or her presentation skills — how well they can communicate the solution. They must spend time outside the classroom developing these skills. Their grade depends on it."

Because of these extracurricular activities and the focus on presentation, the average A&M engineering student takes more than five years to get his or her bachelor's degree. Time well spent according to Moore, who believes engineering education should be modified to be more in line with the schools of architecture, law and medicine — a four-year undergraduate degree (in anything) followed by a two- or three-year master's (or professional) degree in engineering. "It would certainly turn out engineers much more in tune to the world around them, which is an advantage young architects and lawyers have over engineers," he stated.

It is interesting to note that, in surveys of engineering graduates, recent grads wish they had taken more technical courses in college. After ten years of experience, they regret not getting more schooling in business and management. After twenty or more years, they are more likely to say they wish they had studied more literature, history, art and philosophy.

In a letter-to-the-editor (*Engineering Times*, June 1997), Robert Ferrell, a 1948 graduate from Auburn University, summed it up pretty well: "I took my electives all in the engineering field and was a narrow-based graduate. I found out fairly soon that I had to go to college at night to get courses in business finance, business law, organizational management and so on." Ferrell, a mechanical engineer who has a Ph.D. and M.B.A., said, "If you are ever going to rise above being 'just an engineer,' you certainly need to broaden your base."

Lee Iacocca, former head of Chrysler and a graduate mechanical engineer, reflected: "In my day, they tried to make you specialists. And not knowing any better, I believed that was the smart way to go. I was one of those science snobs who looked down my nose at liberal arts majors. Why does anyone need to study liberal arts? Well, I've finally realized what they were driving at." Specialists may have a lot of facts at their disposal, he says, but "it doesn't help them think."

It is time to seriously consider two types of engineering degree programs: one, a four-year, purely technical degree plan, for those who truly only want to be a technical engineer or technician in the future. And another that is more in line with (and equivalent to) a degree in law or medicine, for those who want to lead — want to be professionals of equal standing with doctors and lawyers and architects. In his Centennial Address, Augustine remarked: "One needs more training to give my neighbor's basset hound a vaccination than one needs to design a structure upon which the safety of thousands of people depend."

He and Walter Moore, as well as many other well-known authors on the matter such as Florman and Athanasios Moulakis, author of *Beyond Utility*, have made insightful proposals on educating tomorrow's engineer. Augustine suggests that a five- to six-year course of study is needed for a degree in engineering, one that has these six basic elements: 1) An emphasis on the basics; 2) Development of team skills; 3) Exposure to the political process; 4) Development of communications skills; 5) Greater emphasis on "systems engineering;" 6) Instruction about the international world — because "the 'global village' has arrived."

Florman, though he would not be against the five- to six-year concept, gives it little hope for materializing unless industry "plays its part by starting to compensate engineers appropriately for the additional investment of time and the additional talents developed" in a longer program. For now, he suggests what can be done "is for each institution to reassess its current programs, to craft new ones featuring a basic four-year curriculum as rich and inspiring as it can be, and to encourage students to pursue at least a one-year master's degree."

In a similar vein, Moulakis, who heads a special Humanities for Engineers Program at the University of Colorado, proposes that a four-year program could be effective if more thought went into the selection of non-technical courses. He reports: "Typically, a haphazard selection of social science and humanities courses produce meager educational results." On the other hand, he says, "An engineer who has enjoyed a broad exposure to liberal learning and who has had the opportunity to lay a solid foundation in the humanities will be 1) a fuller and richer human being; 2) a better citizen; 3) a more useful, effective and successful person; and, finally, perhaps surprisingly, a better engineer."

The points made by all four have merit. However, the only answer I see is to have the two different degree plans I mentioned earlier: a four-year truly technical degree, void of any non-technical subjects (so students can get it in four years instead of four-and-a-half or five-years), and a six- (or seven-) year combined bachelor's/master's (or professional) degree program similar to those for law, medicine and architecture (so engineers can legitimately stake a claim that theirs is a learned profession — and that we do have as much education as the person prescribing pills to basset hounds.)

WHAT NEEDS FIXING?

If engineers can resolve their education problem — and address the concerns of both the purely technical engineers and of those who want to be leaders, actively involved in society — what needs to be solved? What issues should engineers be outspoken about? What road forks do we face?

Most agree the U.S. has moved from a manufacturing-based to a services-based economy, and many believe we face a shortage of people who can create wealth and a surplus of those who would divide wealth. Well-known business leaders, engineers like Iacocca and Jack Welch of General Electric, have been outspoken for some time about our future in the global marketplace because we manufacture less and less in this country every year.

Bob Derecktor, a master shipbuilder from Newport, RI,

probably hit the nail on the head best when he expressed his concern about the U.S. losing much of its shipbuilding and high-tech manufacturing to Pacific Rim countries: "I don't think we have enough sense in this country any more to recognize just what's happening to us. It's like the fall of Rome. In this country, we are salesmen and administrators and lawyers. And Asians are production people and engineers and designers."

Former Colorado Governor Richard Lamm, who now is Co-Director, along with former Colorado Sen. Hank Brown, of the Center for Public Policy and Contemporary Issues at the University of Denver, has long prophesized that the countries having the best wealth creators — engineers, scientists and technicians — will in the long run have the most robust economies and be the strongest nations.

Welch reminds us "that without its engineers, Japan would never have become the world economic power it is today." Iacocca states that "there is such a thing as an economic food chain, just like the one in nature. And it starts at the bottom with people growing things or building things. Someone in the pond has to produce something or pretty soon everyone in the pond dies." In his book *Talking Straight*, he points out: "With the shrinkage in manufacturing, 76 percent of our labor force is now in the service sector. Now, that 76 percent may work pretty hard, but they don't do much toward solving our trade problem."

So while lawyers and middlemen are one of the fastest growing segments of our population, production people — the wealth creators — are decreasing in large numbers. Since 1986, the number of engineers graduating each year in the U.S. has dropped — by some 19 percent, almost 15,000 persons. While the U.S. has twice the population of Japan, we graduate 25 percent fewer engineers each year.

In our engineering colleges, foreign-born students who

are seeking graduate (Ph.D.) degrees now outnumber our own; they are learning skills they will, in large measure, take back to their own countries, while we are increasingly becoming a technologically illiterate nation.

Can we reverse these trends? Can we do anything to get more of America's youth to become engineers and scientists?

We as a nation seem to be — or at least the media tells us such is the case — infatuated with celebrities and money. We are constantly reading and hearing about rock stars, movie stars, sports figures, and even lottery winners and get-rich-quick schemers. Rarely does the press recognize people who create things and make ideas a reality — those who produce, achieve and add value. They say those kinds of things are not news — that scandals and murders are news. I disagree.

NATIONAL HEROES

Our national heroes and role models ought to be those who make millions of lives easier, explore the universe, build new facilities for a cleaner, better world, etc. Where are some of the builders and producers we had in the past — engineers like John and Washington Roebling, whose Brooklyn Bridge is still one of the most beautiful and utilitarian structures in the world, over a 100 years after it was built? Why aren't the likes of Alexander Graham Bell, Henry Ford, Thomas Edison and Buckminster Fuller (inventor of the geodestic dome) — as well as the thousands of unnamed engineers who keep the country moving toward a better future — highlighted in the media?

We need the likes of William Shockley, co-inventor of the transistor — one of the greatest inventions of the 20th century, and G.W. Goethals, the engineer of the Panama Canal, who President Teddy Roosevelt said (to his own amazement) was not only an outstanding engineer but also someone extremely well-versed — an intellectual who could speak on important worldly matters.

Leaders in the wealth-creating fields like engineering must step forward and be recognized. Our future standards of living depend on them. All the movie stars, sports heroes or middlemen — no matter how much money they make individually — do little, if anything, to improve these basic needs of life. Nor do they create new ideas and products to enable us to compete in the new world order and the emerging global economy.

Many of these needs are steeped in technological content. They range from such challenges as energy production and transportation to health care, environmental cleanup, national security and economic competitiveness. The companion action which must be taken is eliminating widespread technological illiteracy among those educated in the liberal arts and holding high-level, decision-making positions. There is a danger to all when those to whom we entrust our well-being do not understand even the rudimentary aspects of critical engineering issues.

THE WILL TO DO IT

We could be moving forward with many advances, if the public support for them — like the Kennedy-inspired moon landing — could become a reality. We have the technology to send people to Mars, to construct a bridge between Alaska and Russia, to make a supersonic jet transport superior to the Concorde, to erect a mile-high building and to build a superconducting supercollider.

Likewise, we could substantially increase the output of America's energy from nuclear power, creating a steady stream of safe, non-polluting power for this country, as is being done today in Europe and Japan. But too many organized groups in the U.S. resist it and will continue to block the use of nuclear power. Similarly, we could open new oil fields in Alaska or off-shore, but there is public resistance to that as well. The engineering know-how is there, but politically there is no will to do so.

The public must be convinced there is a need for (and be willing to fund) such things. And engineers should be leading the debate on whether any or all of them are beneficial to progress. Are they safe? What impact will their development, or lack thereof, have on everyone's quality of life? Some — maybe many — from our ranks are required to be in the thick of things, leading the public debate on these issues.

LAWSUITS AND INNOVATION

We could build automated highways that would increase convenience, reduce accidents and last twice as long as our current ones, but who will pay for them? And in today's litigious climate, who is going to insure the engineers and builders who design and construct them?

Engineers must get involved in those public debates addressing frivolous lawsuits because they prevent innovation and advancement. In their 1996 Comprehensive Professional Liability Report, the American Consulting Engineers Council reported that, even though insurance costs are down slightly, consulting engineering firms pass up using new materials and techniques because of fear of lawsuits. Fifty-four percent of our nation's consulting engineers resist trying innovative approaches because of the threat of the liability for doing so.

THE LEGACY

America will always need technically competent engineers to design new products and systems, and the built-environment*. But as General Hank Hatch (Ret.), former head of the U.S. Army Corps of Engineers, states, "We must seek out those amongst us with the talent and breadth to engage in the debate." Otherwise, many forward-moving concepts will wither on the vine.

Hatch, a three star general, is now president of Fluor Daniel-Hanford, and the current president of the World Engineering Partnership for Sustainable Development. As such, he is a leading spokesman on sustainable development globally. He says, "We must celebrate those who are broader citizens and encourage them to join in public discourse."

As I stated earlier — as I have said for years — engineering is more than a useful and beneficial profession; it is vitally essential. But — there's always a "but" — we make the things that other people run. For the engineering profession of tomorrow to be a learned profession having equal stature with architecture, medicine and law, a career choice attractive to our brightest and most talented youth, and a significant force in directing the world's future, we must successfully deal with the forks in the road we now face.

The legacy of engineering is everywhere. Its destiny must be in leadership.

(*Footnote: Built-environment is anything mankind builds above or below ground — buildings, bridges, towers, dams, roads, tunnels, harbors, pipelines, etc. — or that it modifies in nature.)

2

MINISKIRTS & MEMORIES

*"Men acquire a particular quality by
constantly acting in a particular way."*
—Aristotle

I have come to many forks in the road over the course of my career, and, as Yogi Berra suggested, I generally took them. Truth be told, however, like most young people I didn't think at the time that my actions and experiences would all become the building blocks for my vision of the future. It occurred to me, though, that as I set forth my views in writing over the years — and now in this book — a look back at where I have been helps give that vision context.

I could offer a resume and list all the projects I have worked on, but that two-dimensional stuff sums up the parts of a life without considering the exponential whole. Memories only live between the lines of the stark list of accomplishments, yet they are the very things that shape the person. Like all engineers, I studied the sciences and mathematics and the intricacies of building and creating. But it was where I was, who I was with and what happened along the way that made it all interesting and enlightening.

I offer these memories of a life in engineering and business as the basis for my way of thinking. These personal anecdotes shaped my outlook and philosophy of how engineers fit into and impact the bigger picture.

THE FIRST YEARS

My father was a general contractor on the plains of Eastern Colorado and, as a child, I thought I might want to do that too. I admired my father and thought he was important because he constructed big schools, churches and college buildings. I worked for him while I was growing up.

However great my affection for my father, I often noted that the architect (or engineer) who would come out to the job site would often instruct my father on the proper way to do things. That person seemed even more important to me. I suppose every son wants to do his father one better, so while I was still in high school, I decided to become an architect (or architectural engineer). My dad thought this aspiration was great, but ironically another father, my parish priest, was dismayed. As his best Latin student, he thought the priesthood was more my calling.

I was called, however, less by the spiritual than the structural, so I enrolled in the University of Colorado to become an architect. It took barely a semester, though, to doubt my architectural design talents. I then made what was to be the most momentous decision of my professional life: I crossed the campus and enrolled in the CU College of Engineering where I thrived and never looked back. There I discovered my real talent, my real calling, and all the structure — and structures — I would ever need.

My first job, right out of college, was with the U.S. Bureau of Reclamation which, at that time, had 1,000 engineers in its

Denver design office. It was good pay and great training, but after four years as a G-man I felt the tug of free enterprise and the beckoning of the world of small business. I became, once and forever, a consulting engineer.

(One of my very good friends from the government days stayed with the bureau throughout his career. Now he is happily retired and playing a lot of golf. I'm still working very hard. Sometimes I wonder why he was smarter than me.)

At first, I worked for another consulting engineering company, a very good firm. I discovered I loved the excitement of the profession and was happy being a consultant.

However, I'm not truly content if I'm not in charge and I didn't like working for someone else. My father had his own business, as did his father, and as did my great-grandfather. Plus, I was young and didn't know all the problems that lay ahead, so I founded my own consulting engineering firm. That was in 1966 but it seems like yesterday. Time flies when we really like what we are doing. Or, as Confucius said, "Choose a job you love, and you will never have to work a day in your life."

AN EARLY MENTOR

During our early practice, my firm designed a lot of schools. Those were the days in the middle '60s, when I thought, "Boy, wouldn't it be great if I could net $12,000 a year — I couldn't spend that much money even if I bought everything I ever wanted." Now we feel lucky if we can hire an assistant receptionist at that salary.

Our first two large projects built in late 1966 were college buildings with construction costs of $16 per square foot, including air conditioning. My dad's firm was low bidder on one of the projects, the College Union Center at Northeastern

Junior College in Sterling. Paul Penner's company built the other one, the Humanities and Fine Arts Building, on the same campus.

Lloyd White, with Lincoln Steel, first introduced me to Hinde and Laurinat Architects who, at the time, were designing about every school in western Nebraska. Lloyd, a salty and wise old guy who had been selling steel to my father for years, always used to tell me, "There are a few 'bad actors' out there who will do you wrong. Just remember, if you want to be in business a long time, 'treat people right.' They'll be loyal to you. The bad ones will most likely be at your mercy sometime before it's over."

I took his advice, not really understanding what he meant. But as the years have unfolded, Lloyd White proved to be prophetic many times over. I have always instructed my people to "treat people right" no matter what, and those few bad people I did run into sure enough ended up needing me. (That adage "What goes around, comes around" has truth to it.) I suppose I could have taken great pleasure in the comeuppance. But truth be told, the greatest joy was knowing my reputation for integrity was always solid.

MINISKIRTS AND BASEBALL

My first visit to Hinde and Laurinat's office was spectacular. It was over a camera shop and a sporting goods store in a small Nebraska town. I finally found the door and the stairway up to their space.

The first person to greet me was this extremely good-looking blonde receptionist. She immediately got me coffee and showed off her legs — those were the days of the miniskirt (and hers was one of the shortest ever) — and in a few minutes returned with one of the partners.

He talked for about five minutes and I didn't hear a thing he said. My senses were dulled by the long, dusty drive from Denver and, of course, I was more than a little preoccupied by the blonde.

Thus began a business relationship between our firms that has lasted to date. The blonde has long since gone, but Bob Hinde — head of the firm and an ex-marine and semi-pro baseball player with boundless energy — proved to have the stuff of a lasting friendship, both personal and professional. Together we did more schools and rural hospitals than I can count, but I'll always remember a certain Hyannis, Nebraska bid opening.

The construction bids came in over budget, $14.98 per square foot, for a completely air-conditioned, modern, new high school. It seems a bit ridiculous now with construction costs where they are, but in those days, 1969, the owner was not pleased. I'm glad Bob was a good talker and reasoned the school board into a better mood so we could leave town in one piece. Without his steady hand and glibness, I may have never been able again to face a government committee on a bid.

DEEP POCKETS AND LAW

I'll always remember the day the incorporation lawyer walked into our office. We'd been in practice for a couple of years and were making a little money, and he said, "You need to protect your personal assets. You need to be a corporation." Before the ink was dry on the by-laws, I was contacted by an insurance man — how do they learn about these things so fast?

He promptly sold us on errors and omissions and valuable papers, etc., insurance to protect the corporation. Now we were protected, and at a small cost. In those days, insurance premiums were like interest rates: small numbers.

What we didn't know was that lurking out there was a "sleeping giant," litigation, and we didn't know a thing about the "deep pocket" theory.

I have, of course, since learned more than I wanted to know about the concept of deep pockets: someone is "wronged," he gets a "payoff" from someone. In the "deep pocket" theory the courts say, in effect, "Our number one concern is that the parties hurt are treated equitably. We will get the money to do that from whichever party we can." Who is at fault usually has little, if anything, to do with who makes the "payoff" — it's more a matter of whose money is the easiest to tap.

Your insurance, designed to protect your assets and your corporation's assets, has suddenly become the client's, a contingency fund if you will. You ask if they would like to help pay any or all of the premium, and you are greeted with hysterical laughter.

Likewise, fee retainers are not retainers at all; they are the amount of fee, normally 10 percent, that certain clients keep because your drawings and/or specs (specifications) are not perfect. At typical, average billing rates (in 1980) of $50 per hour for you and your staff — attorney's and accountant's fees are at $100 or $200 per hour — you are expected to be perfect. No one, not even John Elway, the Denver Broncos' star quarterback at a six-million-dollar-a-year salary, is perfect. I don't recall hearing of him paying damages to the fans when he throws interceptions.

REBAR AND HIGH TENSION

My favorite court cases include being named in a lawsuit because a laborer at a construction site (unwisely) picked up a rebar to push a high tension power line out of the way so a piece of construction equipment could clear the line. Workman's compensation did not provide his survivors (and their attorneys) with enough money. So since everyone knows rebar is structural, let's get money from the architect's structural engineer. The case was quickly dismissed, a credit to the wisdom of the courts. Or was it because the owner had "deeper pockets?"

In another favorite case, a drunk slipped on the ice going out of the rear delivery door of a building, two buildings down from one on which we were the structural engineers. There was no architect on the building where the drunk slipped and the architect for our building was retired and living in Florida, so we were named. It cost us $2,000 in legal fees to get the suit dropped. We were advised we would have little chance at a counter-claim for a frivolous lawsuit, which has always amazed me.

Attorneys at $200 an hour (1980s' rates) do not need to know, for instance, the difference between a mechanical or structural engineer. So when you're named in a lawsuit because the air conditioning or mechanical system doesn't work, you can't bring a frivolous lawsuit against the lawyer. The courts typically say, "Legal experts only know law — not engineering or construction," so lawyers can name as many people as they want as defendants without real fear of reprisal.

This is wrong! Something has to change, probably at the legislative level. Litigation is strangling the American business world and everyone pays for that. Some doctors refuse to deliver babies and surgeons are more concerned about how their procedures will be interpreted at a trial than about the medical techniques of the operation. We live in a cover-your-tracks syndrome. We need to be responsible for our actions, to be sure, but perfection is out of the question. We should also be adequately compensated for this responsibility; nothing more and nothing less.

SQUARE, SIX-SIDED OR OCTAGONAL

One time a structural engineer was an expert witness for an owner in a lawsuit involving pre-engineered metal storage tanks that collapsed during a wind storm. The tanks were improperly designed and installed but, more seriously, the anchor bolts were all wrong: they were not embedded in the concrete foundation when it was poured so expansion bolts were substituted.

This required drilling four inches into the concrete for five-inch-long, expansion-type bolts — which the installer found to be hard work. He came up with an ingenious solution to save time: he only drilled 1-1/2 inches into the hard concrete and used 2-1/2 inches of stacked washers. The bolts only had thread at the ends so he needed all the washers to screw the nut tight enough to attach the tanks to the foundations. It didn't take the pesky, old, plains winds of western Nebraska long to display the folly of this time-saving connection.

At his deposition, the engineer was questioned long and hard by the opposing attorney. "Fact finding to confuse the expert" questions were rapidly put forth, questions such as, "Were the expansion bolt nuts square, six-sided, or octagonal?" and "Have you ever designed a corn storage bin with these exact dimensions, at this exact site before?" and "How many formal college courses did you take that dealt exclusively with anchor bolts for farm structures?" and "Does wet corn weigh more than dry wheat?"

Four hours later, the opposing attorney did make the mistake, in closing, of asking the engineer his opinion. In 15 minutes of non-stop response — not without the attorney's objections or attempts to silence — he detailed the problem thoroughly.

The corn storage case was settled out of court and to the advantage of the engineer's client.

MOON WALK AND BUILDING PERMITS

In 1969, two U.S. astronauts were the first men to walk on the moon. While millions watched on TV, architect Jerry Seracuse and I were trying to get a building permit in Chicago, in many ways a more difficult assignment.

It was back when Montgomery Ward was expanding and building several stores in regional centers throughout the country. We were their "Colorado connection."

Seracuse's firm, Seracuse Lawler Partners (SLP), was the architect, we did the structural engineering, and Craftsmen Construction was building the stores using precast furnished by Rocky Mountain Prestress (RMPS). All of us were based in Denver. RMPS was shipping concrete double-tees from Denver all over the place, including to Fresno, California.

A typical day would be: line up our men, fly to Chicago arriving at 11:00 a.m., work until 6:00 p.m., catch a plane back to Denver, sneak in a few hours of sleep, meet with our office, catch the mid-morning flight to L.A., switch planes to Fresno, do some work there, then basically redo our schedule in reverse order. Where is the energy of youth? I get tired just thinking about it now.

Around this time, my firm, Richard Weingardt Consultants, Inc., (RWC) had three offices — one in Lincoln, Nebraska, one in Sterling, Colorado and one in Denver — and a full-time company pilot for our own airplane, leased with the option to purchase.

Once we flew the single-engine Beechcraft to Chicago for a meeting, got caught in a storm, our wings iced up, and we had to land in a fog at the little Meigs Field on the edge of Lake Michigan in downtown Chicago. I never got in that plane again — I've flown commercial ever since. I think a lot about Neil Armstrong taking a giant leap for mankind on the moon at the very same time I chickened out of general aviation and took a few small steps over to the United Airlines counter.

SAUDI ARABIA VIA ROME

Shortly after the business recession of 1973-75, we became involved in several projects in the Middle East. My first trip to Saudi Arabia was barely less than frantic.

I was vacationing with my family in the Mediterranean when our client called. The first group of projects for which we had negotiated a fee was "ready to go — right now!"

I was to meet the architect, Paul Pierson of SLP, in Geneva to pick up my visa. Upon arriving there, we were informed that the Saudi visa office was in Bern, which has no airport. We frantically drove there, but the Saudi embassy was closed so we had to stay over that night.

The next morning, after a two-hour wait, we picked up our visas and were notified that our meeting in Jeddah had been postponed two days. This was great since I could return to Nice, properly bid my family adieu and pick up more of my luggage. Paul accompanied me.

On the day of our departure, three hours before flight time, we discovered that both Paul and I needed smallpox booster shots — panic! In France (at that time), this was not a small chore. We needed to pick up the vaccine at a pharmacy, then take it to a doctor's office. With only two hours until flight time, we had a real sense of urgency: Paul with his socks sticking out of his quickly packed suitcase, my wife frantically setting up a doctor's appointment, and the three of us scurrying around Nice to find the smallpox vaccine at a French pharmacy. We asked for it mostly in sign language (none of us could speak French).

We made our flight with minutes to spare. Paul and I had to switch planes twice, in Rome, then again in Athens — and some place along the line they lost all of my luggage. To this day, I have never seen it.

We walked into the meeting in Jeddah right on time by

Arabian time: 30 minutes late. Our business went well and the trip to Saudi Arabia proved successful, but I personally had a difficult time. I had only the few clothes from my carry-on case and had to purchase odd assortments of toiletries.

I also lost my appetite, but this proved a godsend because it forced me into a needed diet to shed a few extra pounds. The lack of food, along with the sauna-like high temperatures and humidity, caused me to lose, in one week, 12 pounds and an inch around my waist. Some Greek baggage handler probably had to bulk up to wear my lost clothes.

ABOUT LOW FEES AND SERVICE
Or the trials and tribulations of a private engineering business.

On getting the job, limited services, low fees and trying to make a profit: If you own your own businesses, you have heard the following standard "lines" while being interviewed as the designer for a project: "Have you ever designed one just like this, at this exact site, with this exact budget, with this exact team before?" or "This will be the tallest of its type in the world — how many have you designed just like it?"

Your competition is a large firm with 500 people (and even though the project can only have three people working on it at peak time), you are asked, "How do we know you can get it done as effectively as they?"

Or, your competition is a small office of six people (and it will take 20 people full-time for the next 12 months to complete), and they ask, "How can we be assured we'll get 24-hour-a-day participation by a principal?" And the list goes on.

In reality, they'll probably give the job to a predetermined firm, selected long before you went through the motions of an interview or made a response to their RFP (request for proposal).

"You mean because you only had six weeks to do three month's work and because we told you our brother-in-law will be the contractor, so keep the details to a minimum since he knows what he is doing, and your fee should be half a normal fee, and you are telling us you will not buy that angle-iron lintel that the brother-in-law forgot to price in his bid?"

Translation: we would like you to help pay for our project but you do not get to own any of it — and we don't want you to make any money designing it.

ACCOMPLISHMENT

Each year, since our founding in 1966, RWC celebrates our anniversary with a real sense of accomplishment. Our firm is quite proud of its completed work, which includes numerous national award-winning designs and even a few significant foreign jobs.

It is fulfilling to look back at so many successful projects, satisfied clients and the events that happened along the way. It is also exciting to look forward to the future, to the 21st century. Our firm has matured nicely. My partners, along with our staff, are youthful, aggressive and hardworking, with fresh new ideas.

Fifty percent of our projects come from outside of Colorado. We can see the day — in the next millennium — when work in foreign countries will be a significant part of our business.

I have, however, reflected on my own 38 years as an engineer. For the last dozen years, I have been seriously questioning the profession's role in society. I see that engineers are called on to make things run, but not to run things.

What can be done to correct this? How can the profession better attract the brightest and best? None of my three children, now grown and on their own, became an engineer; one is a financial controller, one is an artist, and my oldest daughter is a lawyer (which I do not hold against her since she is in international business law, not in litigation). It is with sadness, however, that I must note the continuous generations of my family's involvement in the design and construction industry will be broken with me when I retire.

That is why I wrote this book. It's my progeny, if you will. It is my, and I'm sure the reader's, wish to leave a great legacy so those who come after us will have the opportunity to be even greater than we were.

I do not come to this task unprepared. I learned early that to get ahead in the consulting engineering business I had to get as deeply involved as possible in engineering professional organizations. I then learned how helpful it is to get involved in other, related organizations, so I made myself visible in the architectural and construction communities.

Then it dawned on me I really needed to get even more visible, so I connected with local and state politics, and became involved in various chambers of commerce and other general-business community organizations.

I also found out that when I write articles for newspapers and magazines outside of the engineering world, even more visibility comes along.

I did these things, at first, for business reasons, and it worked. I probably became the most visible engineer in Colorado. It did, indeed, make the phone ring more often or, at the very least, make it easier for me to have my own phone calls answered or returned. I became, frankly, someone to reckon with.

But soon I discovered that the world is run by politicians, lawyers, developers, bankers and community leaders. They often operate without sufficient input from the very people who would eventually be called upon to make their plans work: engineers. I looked around and saw a reticence, even an unwillingness, among my fellow engineers to step forward and enter the debate. We were, I concluded, truly the people who knew how to make things work, but not typically the people called upon to lead or run the show. I decided to be different.

Over the years, I have entered the debate. I have served on numerous state and local government councils and commissions. I have put an engineer's point of view, I believe, into many decisions on public policy.

ENGINEERING ASSOCIATIONS

But to be truly effective, I knew that I had to find other engineers of like mind to bolster our cause, and to counsel even more than to take part. In this regard, I have served in a number of leadership positions in our state engineering organizations, including a stint as president of a couple of them. Next, I served on the executive committee of a national association representing the consulting engineering industry, the American Consulting Engineering Council (ACEC), for several years.

And I am proud to say that I served the 1995-96 year as national president of ACEC, where my professional vision was manifested in the theme of the "Four I's: Imagination, Involvement, Information and Impact." This initiative resulted in the publication of the ACEC book *Seeing Into The Future.* I have had more than positive feedback on it from my engineering colleagues throughout the world. I feel confident that our ACEC message is now busy creating engineering visibility and leadership locally, nationally and internationally.

One last reflection. Near the end of my term as ACEC president, I took a few days off my incredibly busy schedule to have a small medical procedure for an insignificant but nagging problem. In preparation for the procedure, doctors discovered I had a far more serious situation to face, and that very day — which I had expected to be uneventful — I had emergency open-heart surgery. It saved my life.

But more than that, the surgery *changed* my life. Oh, yes, now I eat better and take better care of myself with exercise and all that. The experience, however, strengthened my resolve. It proved to me that change — in one's lifestyle, in one's thinking — is not to be feared but embraced. If anything, nearing death showed me that life has more than meaning; it has purpose.

3

RUNNING THINGS

"I don't think much of a man who is no wiser today than he was yesterday."

—Abraham Lincoln

In virtually every language in the world, the word for the person who does engineering is distinct, specific and celebrated. In the English language, however, it is quite fuzzy. The word "engineer" can be used to define a wide array of occupations: all the way from the professional engineer (who actually does engineering and typically has, at the minimum, a bachelor of science degree) to someone who operates engines or machines, or drives trains. No wonder the public is confused. No wonder, when quizzed or polled, many American citizens indicate the term "engineer" means a person who runs a train.

Sadly, it is not just that many in the public do not know what engineers do; it is that in their mistaken identity they think of us as being in charge of the train. If we did work on the railroad, we wouldn't be the engineer running the train; we'd be the fireman keeping it running.

People who really understand the engineering profession — including us, the engineers — know only too well that we make projects run but we don't run them.

Other people, politicians, lawyers, business and community leaders, actually run things. They make the policy decisions that lead to public works projects, and they are often quick — and entitled — to take public credit for new roads, bridges, convention centers and airports. These same types of people usually call the shots in the manufacture of products and on private development. They are responsible for their communities' office buildings, business parks, shopping centers, subdivision communities and factories. All of these projects — public and private — create a context for people: transportation, manufacturing, housing, employment and, ultimately, prosperity.

These other people — mostly non-engineers — shape our physical environment and set our policy agenda. They get involved. They have vision. They take on leadership roles and run our communities. And they hire engineers to make sure they are run properly.

NOBLE CALLING

Engineering is a noble calling. We create wealth and help maintain the standard of living for everyone. We turn ideas into reality; a design into a product like a building, bridge, car or space ship; a computer chip into a machine that does something.

Still, many people aren't aware we do these things. Engineers just go about their work — do a good job with little or no fanfare — making our highways safer to drive on, purifying the water we drink, cleaning up the environment, solving hazardous waste problems and designing new products, systems and facilities.

We take remote inventions or scientific creations and fashion them into something useful. Yet we are an invisible profession and engineers are quiet — a silent group in a world increasingly dependent on advanced technologies.

We desperately need to change this state of affairs. We need to move up the economic "food chain." Not only must we offer the country and the world our expertise as engineers in making things run, we must become much more involved in running things. Our involvement can and will, ultimately, benefit us as individuals and our profession at large. We also truly have a great deal to offer our communities and our world. To get engineers involved in leadership in society, they have to get concerned with and involved in the "big picture" — the broad societal issues that are the bases of leadership.

Joe Barton, the senior member of the group of three professional engineers (P.E.s) in U.S. Congress, put it right on the line when he told us that, if we want to make the world better, we must get involved. He challenged the engineering community "to get involved in the political arena." He said that if you believe in something strongly enough it will, many times, mean, "You'll have to debate people you disagree with." This will require exposing "your ideas and expertise" to public scrutiny, so you must be able to see the "big picture" impact of issues. According to Admiral Hyman Rickover, "father" of the nuclear submarine, this means, "in addition to technical expertise," engineers must "have good training in the liberal arts and understand the world around them."

"Engineers have often asked: why don't the U.S. president and our foreign embassies have engineering advisors? Some have asked why engineers are assumed to be included by the United Nations and most broad global organizations in the category of science and technology," reported James Poirot, the 1994-5 president of the American Society of Civil Engineers (ASCE), in an editorial about sustainable development matters (in *Engineering News Record*). Poirot's explanation: "It's because we are absent from the policy-making processes."

NOW IS THE TIME

There's no time like the present for us to make our move. We have just had our last two national presidential elections before the next century and, during both, major campaign issues addressed American productivity, competitiveness and leadership. In 1991 during his first run for the White House, President Bill Clinton talked a great deal of creating jobs for Americans and bringing the means of production — the foundation of wealth — back to the American worker.

How successful he was in fulfilling his campaign promises will be debated, but the American economy has regained momentum since he was first elected. He was re-elected in 1996 in an atmosphere of continuing economic expansion. But it will be no simple task to have this trend continue in the modern global economy. It's going to take the creative thinking, technological expertise, unselfish involvement and just plain, simple hard work of leaders from a whole host of professions, trades and business backgrounds — including engineering — to keep it moving.

As has often been said, you either lead, follow or get out of the way. This time, engineers — as individuals and as a profession at large — need to lead. I have some observations, suggestions and directions in the pursuit of that leadership.

THE FOUR DILEMMAS

Whenever consulting engineers get together, we talk about four basic issues or, in our case, The Four Dilemmas:

1. Selection by lowest fee (rather than qualifications)
2. Frivolous lawsuits (high insurance costs)
3. Government regulations (and unfair competition)
4. The public's lack of understanding (awareness) of what engineers do

We have been talking amongst ourselves about these same topics for at least the last 35 years and we're getting nowhere fast. We have, in a very real sense, decided that, because of our education, talent and expertise, we deserve better treatment. But we have done little to effect any meaningful change.

I came across a comment in a national trade magazine for the American Production and Inventory Control Society which hit a nerve. In a column by APICS' International President Donald E. Wilson Jr., he said: "Doing the same things over and over again and expecting the results to change is one definition of insanity."

I have rolled that line over and over again in my mind and I am convinced that we have been practicing a form of insanity. It's not that we should change our ultimate goals; it's that we have to look at the way we have been doing things and figure out more effective strategies of influencing the results.

I propose we get much more pro-active in dealing with The Four Dilemmas. They will not be resolved by talking amongst ourselves and keeping them within the confines of our profession.

We need to take on leadership roles outside the narrow limits of our businesses and our professional associations. We need to move up the "food chain" to where important decisions are made. This is where we will get results.

OTHER PEOPLE'S PROBLEMS

Engineers, especially those in private practice, tend to work for almost every other kind of profession: politicians, lawyers, public administrators, bankers, accountants, industrialists. In a world where technology is more and more the key to survival, this seems out of kilter.

Engineers have become managers of other people's ideas, in effect, their technicians. We design the bridges they tell us to design — when, where and for how much. Very few of us are in positions of authority deciding if we need the bridge, its budget, where it should be located or other issues, such as what environmental concerns are meaningful.

In a way, this is the nature of engineering, especially the consulting engineering business. We consult with and tell people how to solve problems; how to turn their ideas into reality. Many times we merely serve as extensions of our client's staff — departments of transportation, for instance. Because of this subservient position, understandably we are often treated like technicians — one engineering firm is the same as the next, so why not select one over the other merely on price?

The public perception of engineers — and perception is often more powerful than reality — is that we do not have leadership qualities. By not being prominently involved in society, community affairs and politics, we are subject to other people's decisions and legislation. We are forced into re-action instead of action. For example, in several states, Massachusetts, Florida and Connecticut among them, bills have been proposed to raise additional state revenues by taxing services. The proposals specifically exempted lawyers and doctors, but not engineers. There is a night-and-day difference between the lobbying budgets of engineering societies and the American Bar Association or the American Medical Association. And while each of these groups speak with "one voice" for their profession, engineers — with their multitude of organizations — do not.

In Washington, D.C., we have 535 Senators and Representatives — but fewer than a dozen are engineers (and, as mentioned earlier, only three of them are registered P.E.s). The majority are lawyers, and we have a $5.5 trillion national debt!

In Colorado, my home state, only one of the 100 people in our state legislature is a professional engineer. How many serve in your state? I'm sure you can count them on one hand.

These other groups — professional politicians, lawyers and community leaders — run our state governments, U.S. Congress and, in many ways, our country.

When lawyers and middlemen — salespeople, bankers, realtors and M.B.A.'s — make more money, not to mention more momentous decisions, than producers and problem solvers, it's time to make major changes. It's time to get more problem solvers who add value — not litigators and non-producers — into high positions and into leadership roles. At the top of the "food chain."

I'm not proposing we wrench leadership away from other groups, only that we engineers *join* them in leadership. The key to survival and economic strength is tied too closely to modern technology — and technology is advancing too rapidly — to leave the world's direction and major decisions totally in the hands of non-technical people untrained in engineering principles.

MARSHALING LEADERSHIP SKILLS

How can engineers become leaders in society?

We certainly don't have lots of free time on our hands; we're so busy making a living, we barely have time to get our work done. Right?

There's something about engineers from day one: We put in nearly five years of coursework to end up with a four-year undergraduate college (B.S.) degree. Even then we take few (if any) courses about the commercial world or running a business.

But somehow, some way we found time to learn enough about business and management and marketing to operate successful engineering companies, or move into management in industry. Now, somehow, some way, we need to develop our leadership skills.

What is leadership?

Because someone is a celebrity or succeeds at making money, it does not necessarily translate into being a leader. To be a leader one must have the following three characteristics: he or she must look (and act) like a leader, must inspire others, and must cause change.

Warren Bennis, the guru of leadership and past president of the University of Cincinnati, spent several years interviewing and studying leaders. In his book *Leaders — The Strategies For Taking Charge,* he states: "Leadership seems to be the marshaling of skills possessed by a majority, but used by a minority. It's something that can be learned by anyone, taught to everyone, denied to no one."

He also said these five key things about leadership:

1. Leadership is not a rare skill.
2. Leaders are made, not born.
3. Leaders are not necessarily charismatic. (Hope for the engineer!)
4. Leadership does not just exist at the top of an organization.

And, most importantly, he said:

5. All leaders have strong people skills. (They can communicate and motivate their followers.)

All leaders can communicate!!! What a concept!

Also, Bennis, Tom Peters, Peter Drucker and other experts on peak performance, stress the difference between managers and leaders. Managers solve problems. Leaders decide what problems to solve. Managers do things right. Leaders do the right things.

Leaders supervise and direct managers (and engineers and technicians). Engineers tend to make great managers but have limitations when it comes to leadership in society.

As Samuel Florman says in his book, *The Civilized Engineer*, "One of the failings of engineers is they overestimate the power of logic and underestimate the power of emotion." He suggests you can't simply convince people not to be afraid of, for example, nuclear power or flying by quoting statistics. You must reach them emotionally as well.

We are both educated and trained not to make decisions without all the facts. But in most of life's situations, we never get all the facts before we need to make decisions — as in politics. Judgment is crucial when facts are lacking.

It is difficult to develop judgment qualities when one is educated too narrowly. We cannot lead beyond our narrow confines if all we bring to the table is a concern for and knowledge of engineering or technical topics alone. We cannot hope to achieve results for our narrow primary concerns without demonstrating we have more than self interest in mind.

There's nothing wrong with self interest — except when it is exclusive. True leadership is demonstrated by placing self interest alongside the interests of others — showing a broad sense of empathy for shared success and establishing the common ground for progress.

GETTING READY

Getting there demands contact — conversation, discussion, camaraderie — with a much broader cross-section of society in a much broader set of contexts. How do we expect other people to care about our concerns if we know nothing and show little care about theirs?

We need to find ways to broaden our perspectives, stretch our imaginations. There are larger problems than The Four Dilemmas which consulting engineers always talk about including AIDS, world starvation, drug abuse, crime, education — the list is endless.

There are many ways to establish the contacts necessary for true involvement, and I will outline a few. First, however, we must consider adopting the basic skills necessary to affect results. Just being there isn't enough; we must also make an impression, offer a contribution. That takes specific skills.

We need to hone our natural talents in leadership. Take classes (or seminars) in communications, public speaking, writing (English), and even Dale Carnegie-type classes — "How To Win Friends and Influence People." Whatever stops us from speaking out, we must overcome it. We must constantly strive to improve and maximize our communication skills.

Likewise, we must develop a fuller understanding of history, geography, political science, psychology, literature and the arts. Become an expert at something outside of engineering. Find a mentor. Just as we have mentors in our engineering careers, we need to find some in society.

Once you look like a leader — once you dress, walk, talk, write and think like a leader — you're ready. For what?

INVOLVEMENT OPPORTUNITIES

It's easy to argue that engineers should get involved but learning what to do, what actions to take, is the most important lesson. I hold no special knowledge nor understanding of exactly the most appropriate actions; I only know what has worked for me and what I see working for others who have emerged as leaders.

These actions are not designed to directly affect The Four Dilemmas or bring an immediate financial return on the investment of time. And it does take time (and effort) to build valuable relationships. On the other hand, being involved — becoming a leader — is its own reward. I know that my associations with many civic, governmental and societal groups have broadened my thinking and interests, given me invaluable perspectives and introduced me to many wonderful people. I would never have met them by associating only with engineers.

And these involvements have given me the opportunity to talk about engineering to people and audiences who have never been exposed to our profession. They have shown unusual interest in what engineering is all about. In the process, I am accomplishing my self-interested goal of broadening the influence of engineering and of myself. I have discovered so many other rewards, I wonder now why I ever worried about the investment.

So, how do you get involved? I suggest these four areas:

1. Community/Civic Organizations (But don't ignore your professional engineering associations — they are much too important.)
2. Education (Not just engineering schools but education in general. Our future will be in the hands of the young.)

3. Politics
4. Public Communications

(Though we touch on these areas briefly here, we'll go into more detail in following chapters.)

The type of community groups you can get involved with are limitless. Community "think tank" groups, chambers of commerce, neighborhood building committees or planning boards, even service groups such as the Lions, Kiwanis and Rotary provide benefits because they broaden your perspective.

Chambers and other local civic groups — downtown associations, for instance — are particularly interesting. You'd be amazed at how much public policy is set through these organizations. You'd also be amazed by the number of senior business leaders you'll come in contact with. It can often take some time before you climb to the top of the groups like serving on the board of directors. But many subcommittees feature broad cross-sections of the business community that will readily accept new players - particularly an engineer with technical expertise.

These groups often get involved with zoning initiatives, for example, which bring together neighborhood leaders, government officials, financing and real estate interests, transportation representatives, and merchant groups. Their work can often lead to development or redevelopment, and engineers could play a central role.

In the educational arena, we may know what should be changed in colleges to turn out engineers for the business world. But talking about it doesn't change our colleges. Involvement will. Become a member of your local college Advisory Board. Get elected to the Board of Regents. Become actively involved in the campaign of someone else running.

Lecture at schools and colleges (and not just about the

problems engineers have, but how engineering affects every-one). Join in public debates about the American education sys-tem. As a nation, we cannot tolerate the current illiteracy ratio or that our students consistently score at the bottom in stan-dardized math and science tests when compared with other countries.

On the local community scene, get involved with your local school board — even run for a school board position — or neighborhood committees that spring up to discuss elemen-tary and secondary education. Become the leader.

In the political arena, opportunities are limitless. We have got to increase the numbers of technical problem solvers in government and lend some balance to the influence of lawyers and professional politicians.

To paraphrase what Plato said centuries ago: "If intelli-gent people don't get involved in politics they will soon find they are being led by the less intelligent."

You don't have to run for (or hold) public office to make a difference or develop policy. (The topic of engineers as politi-cians is discussed in Chapters Five & Six). Help worthy candi-dates get elected. Once they are elected, stay in contact with them — make sure they are doing their jobs.

How many of you know your local legislator? State Sen-ator? U.S. Senator or Congressman? Get to know them; call them up, talk to them, write them personal letters, see them in their "place of business."

Get appointed to Boards and Commissions such as your state's long-range planning board. Most boards or commis-sions make or influence public policy. In many states, thou-sands of positions on boards and commissions are available. Sadly, in Colorado, only about two dozen professional engi-neers serve on any of them. This is less than one-tenth of one percent of the total number of engineers in the state.

There are many other political opportunities as well. Too

few people — and too few engineers — attend their precinct or county caucuses. At these meetings, parties decide who will run and on what platform.

A final thought on politics; a growing number of initiatives and referenda on state and local ballots have an enormous effect on the profession of engineering.

We passed a tax limitation measure in Colorado, for instance, which now severely curtails infrastructure development in our state. There are obvious reasons why engineers should get involved in either fighting or supporting these proposals during campaign seasons. But less than apparent are the contacts, relationships and coalitions we can build with other people and parties interested in the measures. These contacts can and will lead to other relationships — business, for instance.

The fourth area of leadership involvement — an area where we can truly be pro-active — is as spokespeople for the engineering community. Get the attention of the media. Numerous radio and television talk shows need spokespeople on local issues. In the print media, newspapers and magazines regularly accept guest columns and op-ed pieces. Do not overlook local publications or business periodicals where your published views can reach powerful leaders.

Talk about how engineering and technology affect all facets of peoples' lives — their standard of living. The more people who hear what engineers think (and do), the more powerful our comments and opinions will become. Grassroots activities are the catalyst for many social changes, as the dismantling of the Berlin Wall and the results achieved by MADD (Mothers Against Drunk Drivers) so strikingly illustrate.

THE CHALLENGE

We can no longer let it "be up to someone else" to solve our problems. Leadership must be provided, not just by a few in high office, but by large numbers of leaders in every job, profession and industry — including engineering.

Be leaders in your engineering industry, but also get involved in:

1. Your community
2. Education
3. Politics

And, most importantly,

4. Speak out on issues in society. Be the voice of the engineering community.

Your efforts — your leadership — will cause things to happen and change the course of events. You will improve the future for your profession and for society. You can mold history and control your own destiny if you get involved in solving "big picture" problems.

Society needs your talent and will greatly benefit from your problem-solving skills.

As a caution: Keep in mind that problem-solving skills by themselves are not enough for leadership, and having technical competence does not mean that one possesses sound judgment. Athanasios Moulakis, author of *Beyond Utility*, brings us back to reality by stating it is not merely "the problem-solving engineer as such who belongs in public life, but the well-rounded engineer. What is required is not the mere application of factual knowledge but a personal maturity." This emerges "from the actual exercise of judgment." And this may take some trial and error on your part. You may make a mistake or two along the way but remember: It is only a mistake if you don't learn from it. Do not hesitate to get involved.

I like the way Roland Rautenstraus (the only engineer to ever be president of the University of Colorado) put it: "Don't live in the gray monotone world of attempting to make no errors. If you do, you will end your lives wondering if you ever lived at all — and that would be the greatest of all mistakes." (He, of course, was not talking about doing engineering or making calculations.)

Engineering demands exactness and engineering decisions require most of the facts. Leadership decisions rarely enjoy that luxury. To develop personal qualities of a well-rounded, mature engineer capable of sound judgments and leadership requires active participation. It also calls for dedication to a lifetime of observing, studying and trying to understand the essence of the world we live in and the people who inhabit it. The following essays — chapters — delve into how this can be accomplished.

4

THE RIGHT STUFF

"Those who achieve any excellence commonly spend life in one pursuit, for excellence is not often granted on easier terms."

—Samuel Johnson

Engineers have many reasons to be proud. Ours is a profession with grand traditions, and a history of being responsible for and pro-actively engaged in the creation of wealth, opportunity and advancement. Our communities, countries, and societies worldwide benefit from engineering accomplishments. We have the right stuff.

The trouble is that only we seem to know this. Even though we engineers are aware of the influence we have on the world today and will have on it tomorrow, we have been relatively unknown outside of our own narrow circles. Our destiny is that we will have a great impact on the world around us as we move into the new millennium, but we can have an even greater impact — make even stronger contributions to the future — through greater visibility for engineering. We need to work on our image.

THE IMAGE DEBATE

I've been a engineer now for nearly 40 years. As a kid, it was my dream to build the great structures. As a student at the University of Colorado, it was my passion to learn the great questions. As a practicing professional, it has been my pleasure to solve the great problems, meet the great needs, build the great future. I had a dream, studied hard for it, lived it and enjoyed nearly every minute of it.

Engineering is a wonderful profession. What we do adds value. We design and build the infrastructure of society that is the basis for generating affluence for everyone. Roads and bridges, industrial plants, office buildings, satellites and rockets, computer chips and on and on. Without engineers, the means of production, communications, transportation — indeed, progress itself — would be slow moving.

Yet, a Gallup poll a few years ago showed that 33 percent of Americans think engineers drive trains. Not only that, an even higher percentage do not associate us with the great successes of the century — or throughout history.

In 1996, as an example, when the U.S. celebrated the 40th anniversary of the Interstate Highway System — labeled by many as the greatest *construction* project of the century — there was little mention of engineering and engineers. Likewise, the landing of a man on the moon (in 1969) has been hailed as the greatest *scientific* feat in modern history — again with virtually no mention of engineers and engineering. What a shame.

Engineers are more and more thought of as technicians, not as powerful forces responsible for major achievements, or needed for progress. We do not come to the forefront when the average person on the street thinks of a leader.

We've got an image problem.

At least we in America do. In my travels around the world, I've noticed a higher respect and admiration for engineers in other countries. They are a most esteemed bunch.

Henry Michel, chairman emeritus of Parsons Brincker-hoff, Inc., relates this story: When he was working in Italy a number of years ago, he lived in a compound of four houses. Each place was supplied with maids according to the rank of the home's inhabitant (ranked not by age but by the prestige of the individual's profession). It was a time when not many households in Italy had an electric clothes dryer. One of the perks for the most senior of the maids was not only being assigned to the most prestigious occupant, but also getting the best clothes-lines — the ones with the best sunshine. In Michel's compound lived a doctor, a public official and a lawyer. Michel's maid got the best clothes-lines — so respected were engineers in Europe at the time.

So while we, in this country, suffer from a public perception problem — our maids would not get the best clothes-lines — we have a much more bottom-line concern. It has to deal with the people who know only too well what we do and how talented and competent we are. Public officials, real estate developers, industrial chieftains, architects, even railroad barons, regularly call us in to provide the "how" on their problems and their needs. But that's usually *after* the "why" and "what" have been determined. If we're not sitting in when the agenda is set, we live with that agenda — and that means having other people determine our roles and, often, our fees. And, when these projects get done, we get a small footnote in the credits while the public kudos are showered upon our employers.

This is wrapped up in what Americans think of engineers. Surveys indicate we rate high for honesty, integrity and competence among the various professions and occupations, but we're thought of as stodgy, too technical and too narrow. We're "back-room guys" — not the real policy-makers *but* highly honorable people. Most wouldn't even mind if their daughters or sons married one of us. But for the most part, our names are hidden in the fine print that only we read.

We've got a visibility problem.

VISIBILITY

We engineers have some *real* problems, of course. As a profession, though, we have indeed been stodgy, too technical and too narrow. And, occasionally, even arrogant and aloof. Coming out of our shell can pay some real dividends, especially now with national and international demand for our skills again on the rise.

Increased visibility can nourish and enhance the image of engineers in general, and create more opportunities for the more visible engineers specifically. Being more visible doesn't supplant technical competence. It only enlarges our ability to be heard, and to attract quality clients, obtain quality projects or ventures, and to attract and retain quality employees. The good people will want to work for the good firms, and the good firms will get the bulk of the good work.

In my case, I have found that being visible in my profession and my community has brought me extra personal opportunities and rewards I hadn't counted on. I had a gut-level feeling that visibility would bring me such temporal compensations as more business inquiries and increased business — which it has. But I have also found more personal returns. I've met new friends, broadened my interests, and gained new perspectives on world and community issues.

Because of this visibility, I've had — as have others in similar situations — many opportunities to speak and write about these issues *and* engineering in dozens of professional and general-public forums and publications. The feedback confirms that these efforts have conveyed a deeper appreciation for engineering within and outside the profession.

BROADENING THE SCOPE

Well, okay, increased visibility helps enhance image. Together they pay handsome dividends. How does one improve his or her visibility and image?

Several simple visibility techniques work fairly well and they will be discussed shortly. However, I strongly believe we cannot attack the question of enhancing the image of engineering and the individual engineer until we get involved in the broad concerns of society. How have we done to date?

For the most part, engineers have been quite involved in local and national professional societies, but you see very few engineers in elective office or in any aspect of American politics. Is it any wonder that lawyers wield so much influence on public policy, from the local city level all the way to Washington, when so many of them take the initiative to be a part of the political process? Sure, they are often resented and criticized for it, but we have to admit: they are powerful because they are so involved. (Engineers who are successful lawmakers are presented in Chapter Six.)

This same level of involvement, or non-involvement as the case may be, can be seen in the many civic and service organizations in our cities and states around the country. These groups, as well as chambers of commerce, downtown organizations and economic development entities, reach out into the broader business and civic communities. They offer venues for greater visibility, and for engineers to meet new business contacts and offer an engineering perspective.

It has always amazed me how few engineers are active in these organizations. Part of the reason is an attitude I've noticed among some of my colleagues who say: "I'm too busy running my business (or working) and I don't have the time to waste on nonproductive projects." Frankly, I have found these involvements to be important investments of time; even though I am not billing those hours, they have and will lead to new business. But also, with more engineers involved, the business and civic communities at large will gain a better perspective of our industry. That goes directly to sound image enhancement.

INVOLVEMENT IN THE BROADER COMMUNITY

Any aggressive engineer, having the desire, can get involved in the broader community. There are countless opportunities and venues. A few of the more conventional groups include service clubs — the Lions, Rotary, Optimists, etc. They always seem to have as members a quality selection of local business people with broad concerns — many strongly committed to improving the well-being of the community.

Other activist groups

Other potentially powerful associations providing good exposure and visibility avenues include any number of chambers of commerce organizations, downtown merchant groups, general business groups, state-wide business lobbying organizations, etc. In these you can be as active as you want, serving on committees or any number of subcommittees. My recommendation, however, is not to just serve as a committee member, but as the chair. Be the leader of the group.

Serve on your local school board, city long-range planning board or even a performing arts council (push the envelope a little). For six years, I served on Colorado's Historic Preservation Board — designating structures that are historically significant. Until then the Board was controlled by architects, educators and lawyers. Not surprisingly, few engineering projects — bridges, dams or tunnels — were ever deemed to be significant or ever publicized. Now they are. One person, a single engineer — any one of you — can indeed make a difference and it will improve our professional image.

College advisory councils

Become a voting member on your local engineering college advisory board. The engineer's lifelong image of himself or herself often develops in college. Spend time with the dean and professors of the local engineering colleges. Urge them to instill in their students a sense of pride that they are going to be part of a great and noble profession — engineering: the profession that adds value and is critically needed for building a better tomorrow. Encourage the dean and professor to make sure student's communication skills — speech-making, writing skills — are properly addressed. It's a shame how many good ideas never get accepted because they are presented so poorly. Some engineering leaders suggest, tongue in cheek, "Engineers surely could not naturally be as stodgy as they seem. Someone must have taught them how to be so somber." Let's make sure this isn't happening at our colleges.

Public direction setters

To truly get at the heart of the matter and improve our status, we need to become much more *active as leaders* in policy-making bodies in our communities. How we can do this will be discussed in the next chapter. We will study the ways engineers can impact politics, public-policy and public direction — and help enhance our image and visibility while doing it.

TECHNIQUES

What are some techniques — other than getting involved — to become more visible? I have tried several of these over the years that have worked for me and my company. They will work for you too.

Newsletters

My firm has published a small bi-annually newsletter, *The Nautilus*, for the past 20 years. Occasionally we have produced a special issue on a particular event — e.g., our silver anniversary — that has been larger. But for the most part, our newsletter has been an inexpensive, eight-page publication. In it we discuss community issues from an engineering perspective, comment on outstanding projects, including our own, being constructed around the globe. We've included projects like the new $1 billion Getty Center (L.A.) and the multi-billion dollar tunnel under the English Channel (the Chunnel). We also, of course, talk about what goes on with our company.

We send it to our client base, a cross-section of engineers and architects, contractors and developers; to a variety of community leaders and government officials; and, most importantly, to the news media. Besides generating new business leads, *The Nautilus* keeps us in contact with our clients and inspires calls from the news media — some of which have ended up as stories in newspapers and magazines, and gotten us radio and TV interviews.

The media

Most engineers are familiar with industry professional publications, but broad visibility means connecting with the more general media. Just about every city (small and large) in America has daily and weekly newspapers, as well as monthly magazines with sections devoted to business and commerce, and local public issues. All these publications and section editors look for input. It is relatively easy to get a mention in their pages.

First things first, however. Read the publications and become familiar with them. Nothing infuriates editors more than calls or mail from people looking for coverage who quite obviously know very little about the publication.

Almost all of these publications print simple announcements about promotions and new employees at companies. They all also frequently print short stories about new contracts and awards firms have garnered, usually in "People" or "Awards and Citations" columns. Occasionally, simple announcements, if they really impress an editor, will yield stand-alone stories.

Basic news releases should be kept short, to the point and interesting. Include a good quality photograph, and make sure there is a contact person (preferably a senior member of the firm) with a telephone number displayed prominently on the release. Do not be discouraged if not every one of your releases gets in the paper; editors receive hundreds of these every day and use them as fillers. They often lead to calls about more specific topics when the publication is looking for an "expert" to interview, which makes it worth the effort.

If you want to enhance that "expert" status, which I recommend, go a bit further. Editors of these publications are inundated with requests, but they are always looking for good contacts. Call them, write them, invite them to lunch; let them know who you are and what you do, and be willing to offer perspectives on articles they are developing. You'll be amazed how many times your name will appear in print.

The steps we took to develop a strong media relationship program began years ago with this basic approach: We simply sent a few small news releases to our local daily newspapers. When we made someone a new vice president or principal in the firm, we sent out an announcement that also carried some background information on our firm. Sometimes the announcements ran, sometimes not; sometimes they were cut, sometimes they ran in their entirety, with photographs.

After a while, we felt more could be done. So, we got more serious about what we wanted to accomplish and started to pay closer attention to these publications. We identified the reporters, writers and editors who might be interested in the type of projects we were working on. I called them up, got to know them and I discovered that our news releases helped grease the gears. They at least had concrete knowledge that my firm and engineers existed.

I began to suggest articles on things like infrastructure needs, the usefulness of bridges, the urgency for more highway funds, etc. As we got to know each other, these reporters and I, they would ask us questions in other areas and call us about things I would never have thought of. Sometimes we could not comment for liability reasons or just sheer lack of knowledge. But the important thing was we had created a relationship. And it's funny, once our name started appearing in a newspaper or two where the reporter made us sound like authoritative sources, reporters from the other papers would as well.

The next few steps were made easier by those just mentioned. First, we suggested that in real estate stories, for instance, where the reporters made a habit of mentioning the architect and construction company, they also include the name of the engineers. Lo and behold, it began to happen, more often than not. In the past, the editors/reporters just did not think of engineers and their contributions.

Eventually, I asked and/or was approached by these newspapers and magazines to contribute guest columns on a variety of subjects. Over the years, I have written countless commentaries for the press on issues like crumbling bridges, highway funding legislation, the need for a new airport and the value of commuter rail. Since 1986, every February during National Engineers Week, I have created a piece about the value of engineering for several general-interest publications — the newspapers and magazines my neighbors read.

The next step in our media program took longer, and it worked out even better. My company conducted a survey of our state's engineers, architects, contractors and public officials concerning their rankings of the state's best buildings. We used the results of the survey to produce an article for the largest business magazine in the Rocky Mountain Region — it ended up being their cover story. Subsequently, many newspapers around the state saw the article and ran a version of it or just the list of our 10 Best Buildings/structures. The response — and the coverage — was overwhelming.

We followed this with other surveys — the best bridges, our most significant infrastructure projects, Seven Wonders of the Modern World, economic expectations, for example — and have had our surveys and stories (and opinions) carried in numerous local and national media outlets.

It all starts with relationships and involvement. Once you get to know your local media — the people who work there, the type of coverage they feature, the special sections they have — you'll be amazed how much they need you.

The age of marketing

The methods related to the media are the most important part of the visibility strategy because it is a way to reach so many people. But several others are worth mentioning.

This age of marketing is particularly troublesome for the professions — engineering, medicine, etc. — which have histories where overt marketing was frowned upon. But more and more professionals are discovering the value of even minimum efforts. One of the most important is having a company brochure. Though company brochures are not a new concept, it is a good idea to frequently update yours, making sure it is as competent and attractive as your budget will allow. It generally should include a statement of philosophy, capabilities, key personnel resumes, projects, and something about why you are special. Have these handy as leave-behinds for meetings and as complements to correspondence. Additionally, as the Internet comes of age as an everyday tool, so will the use of company web sites.

Another purposeful technique for visibility/image enhancement is to enter your outstanding projects in all the awards programs you can. Local, regional and national engineering professional groups conduct awards programs regularly, as do non-professional groups. They bestow awards for new buildings/structures, new products, and even such things as Total Quality Management commitments and business ethics.

To win a prestigious award is a real honor and will, in many cases, bring you visibility with a broad audience. Actually just entering these programs often garners you a certain amount of visibility. You won't win for mediocre work, but you won't win if you don't enter. I can't tell you how many times someone — more often not, a community leader — says to me, "Oh, you're the firm that wins all those awards."

Choose a role model

Find a role model (or mentor) whose image and visibility you admire. Just as most of us at certain times in our careers have had professional mentors, the same process works well in the area of image/visibility enhancement. Choose someone you respect in this area and study how he or she gains visibility.

ENHANCEMENT BY ASSOCIATIONS

It's not just individuals or companies that need to get involved. We must encourage our local, state and national engineering professional associations to develop strategies as well. The three main things your association can do to increase the visibility and image of its members (if it is not already doing them) includes:

1. Develop a comprehensive media outreach program

Have your association's key personnel get to know the media — reporters and editors can do a lot to spread the word about us. We need to get to know them on a first name basis. Make sure they have your membership rosters, your list of experts and any material telling what engineers do. The media always looks for a list of experts when reporting or writing their stories. Additionally, find out what kinds of news stories they are interested in and supply association members with the information for op-ed pieces. Remember: the media determines what is news, not us.

2. Embark on a public relations - advertising campaign

AIA (the architect's national association) has had a million-dollar-a-year P.R. campaign underway for several years. Its purpose is to appraise the public of the greatness of architects — and most people are already familiar with architects. A lot of their budget is being spent buying ads and placing stories in major magazines like *TIME* and *FORBES*. (I know of no engineering association that has a budget for P.R. anywhere close to that of AIA.)

Several regional engineering societies in the past, however, have joined together. With modest budgets and lots of donated time by members, they have conducted successful statewide news blitzes — getting a major series of articles published on how engineers impact economies and living standards. These types of news campaigns usually succeed if the stories are primarily about people and secondarily about engineering.*

3. Sponsor seminars on "how to" build image

Produce, for members, manuals and seminars on how to

enhance image and increase visibility. Central to improving the face our profession presents to the public is to have ongoing efforts — to teach engineers how to do it.

THE STAR SYSTEM

Bob Hillier, one of America's leading architects and a vocal proponent of design professionals taking on leadership roles in society, points out that the problem with engineers is we don't have a star system.

Hillier, who owns the fourth largest architectural firm in the U.S., said, "Architects have stars like I.M. Pei, Cesar Pelli, Philip Johnson, Richard Meier and Frank Lloyd Wright." And he noted that architects go out of their way to publicize their stars and their profession, telling about what architects do.

"You engineers," he added, "don't have anyone with name recognition who the public can identify with. You are too reluctant to single out and praise anyone from your ranks."

That's something to think about. I don't know why we tend to be shy or humble in telling about who we are and what we are doing. We significantly contribute to society. We should be popping our buttons with pride and making stars out of the giants in our industry. The names of our most notable engineers should become as well-known by the public as names of the super-star architects.

I'm reminded of the story about three men with wheelbarrows, loading rocks. They say engineers are masters of the obvious, so — which one of these men sounds like an engineer? The story goes:

The first man, asked what he is doing, replies, "I'm hauling rocks." The second man says, "Helping to build a wall." And, finally, the third man says, "We are building a cathedral!"

Well, since engineers are building cathedrals and other

great works, let's say so! Let's not be constrained; let's not slight our importance. Let's describe our work so it sounds as interesting, exciting and significant as it really is.

We're not hauling rocks — we're building — building a better future for everyone.

CHECK-LIST OF THINGS TO DO

Here is a summary check-list of action items (some of which have been addressed in detail in this chapter) that individuals, their companies and professional organizations can do to enhance visibility and improve the engineer's image.

Individuals
1. Get involved in community leadership
2. Serve on your college advisory council
3. Write for general readership publications
4. Make friends with editors and reporters
5. Participate in public speaker groups
6. Lecture at schools and colleges
7. Serve on boards and commissions
8. Run for elected public office

Companies
1. Have first-rate brochures, logo, stationery
2. Produce a company newsletter
3. Create a community service event
4. Enter projects in design excellence programs
5. Send news releases about projects and employees
6. Assist employees in getting published
7. Mail reprints of published articles to public/clients
8. Support worthy political candidates and public policy

Associations
1. Provide the media with a directory of members (experts)
2. Fund a public relations - advertising campaign
3. Sponsor seminars on how to build image
4. Establish a design excellence awards program
5. Present annual awards to media persons
6. Prepare op-ed pieces members can use
7. Publish an association newsletter or magazine
8. Produce a video or brochure telling what engineers do

The point is *be visible* — do good work and, without being pompous, tell the world about it. And expand beyond our profession into the world, showing the general public we are concerned about other people. Mingle with and talk to the average person-on-the-street as often as possible. It may be the only time he or she ever has to learn about what engineers do, or what impact engineering has on their lives.

THOSE WHO ADD VALUE

We have the right stuff to be role models. We are well trained to solve problems in the most useful ways. We add value. Let's not leave the well-being of communities totally in the hands of non-engineers. Let us assume our rightful roles in leadership positions in our communities and society. And let's not be shy about talking about our contributions to modern civilization.

As Brendan Gill, the dean of American architectural writers, was once quoted in a *Detroit Free Press* column as saying: "Engineers are far more important than architects, but architects are kind of movie stars. In point of fact, the things that architects get credit for have been done for them by engineers." Let's make sure we get credit for what we do!

And when we do, I'm sure, our status and the prestige of this profession will make momentous strides upward. Who knows, your efforts at improving the image of engineers might even get us prominently mentioned the next time America celebrates an anniversary of the Moon Landing or the Interstate system.

(*<u>Footnote</u>: Attempts have been made to interest TV networks in doing a series on engineers a` la L.A. Law or ER. These efforts by engineering groups have had no success in the U.S.; however, a few countries like South Africa and Australia have produced some. These series, not unlike the lawyer and doctor ones in the U.S., are more about people — and personal conflicts — than engineering. In a similar vein, efforts to get the U.S. Postal Service to produce a series of postage stamps on outstanding engineers or engineering projects have met with resistance. American engineering societies might want to heighten their initiatives in these areas in the future.)

5

THOSE WHO SHOW UP

*"Farming looks mighty easy when your plow is a pencil
and you're a thousand miles from the corn field."*

—Dwight Eisenhower

With challenges in technological advancements and the struggle of maintaining — and funding — an advancing quality of life in the industrial powers and the developing countries, the value-adding skills of engineers have never been more important to our communities, our country and the world at large. However, engineers are woefully under-represented in the important policy-making bodies and boards, from local levels to the halls of U.S. Congress. Why have engineers, by and large, not been involved enough in the leadership opportunities available to them?

Because the world is run by people who show up. What follows challenges engineers to do just that, show up: get more involved in leadership on any and all levels. Several strategies to accomplish the move into leadership are discussed.

ENGINEERS AS LEADERS

For the last dozen years or so, I have been passionately involved in studying and addressing the issue of engineers as leaders — leaders not just in this industry but leaders in society. I strongly believe engineers must get involved as leaders in the policy-making bodies of our communities, states and country to be consequential.

You will probably think I am a hopeless romantic when I share with you, not only my optimism that this can successfully happen, but something else as well. I actually believe what David McCullough, the historian and prize-winning author, discovered about engineers.

In his books, engineers are the heroes. Just read his histories on the building of the Brooklyn Bridge and the Panama Canal. He writes about the greatness of engineers, our intelligence and problem-solving skills, and how what we do uplifts the human spirit.

But even more significant (and what I must confess I now believe because McCullough says it's true) is that in history a few engineers actually had (and have) a sense of humor.

So there you are: engineers are intelligent, have the right stuff — and even a few among us have a sense of humor. Well, we may just need a sense of humor to sit in on, and even lead, policy-making bodies. But seriously, if engineers are to have any real input in running the world, we need to begin — right now. We must develop plans to get more and more engineers elected to public office (at all levels), appointed to public boards and commissions, and seriously involved in the public discourse on the future directions for our communities, country and the world.

Our expertise, along with our pragmatic approach to dealing with problems, is surely needed. I personally believe we are ready for policy-setting leadership and we can handle it.

READY OR NOT?

Or can we?

There are millions of engineers in the world — ten million around the globe and many more than two million in the U.S. What an awesome potential for power, what an awesome potential for impact, and what an awesome potential for influence in public policy and controlling our own destiny.

Couple this with the fact the world is becoming increasingly dependent on technology and impacted by engineering solutions, you can readily see what I'm getting at. Who is well equipped and trained to deal with the many challenges in an ever-more technological world? Engineers! Engineers from both the private sector and the public sector.

And let's look more closely at the numbers. There are ten million of us but, more importantly, we outnumber lawyers worldwide 10 to 1.

Now, unfortunately most of the world's one million lawyers practice in the United States. In our own country, we only outnumber them around 2 to 1. Not great odds against that pesky group, but still better than having them outnumber us.

So we have to ask ourselves: if there are so many engineers in the world, and if the world so much needs our technical expertise:

- Why aren't we more sought after to fill leadership positions?
- Why aren't our exploits more often headline news?
- Why aren't we more often listened to, and our opinions more often sought after, on issues like environmental concerns, infrastructure investment (or the lack thereof) and technological advancement?

Take the issue of Sustainable Development. President Clinton has a 50-member Blue Ribbon panel for Sustainable Development in America. Why aren't any registered professional engineers, who actually do infrastructure design work, on this panel? Don't they know something about the subject?

James Poirot, the only engineering delegate at the Rio + 5 Forum, the five year follow-up to the United Nation's 1992 Earth Day Summit in Rio de Janeiro, said, "I heard little response when the potentially powerful role of engineers in implementing sustainable development was described. The response was not surprising when the world's engineering associations, representing 10 million engineers, have not had a consistent involvement in the UN's programs, agreements or policy documents." Poirot is a past president of ASCE and former chairman of CH2M Hill.

The answers to these questions — and ultimately the solutions to these dilemmas — are rooted firmly within the engineering community. I believe our lack of recognition as leaders stems directly from "four weaknesses" of our profession:

1. Poor visibility
2. The public's perception of engineers
3. Inadequate involvement in our communities
4. Absence from public direction-setting groups

We delved into the first two of these — visiblity and the public's perception of us — in Chapter Four. We pointed out that, even though engineers contributed enormously to the accomplishment of them, the public seems little aware that engineers had much (if anything) to do with the success of the Moon Landing or the U.S. Interstate Highway System. Both were tremendous engineering achievements.

I believe these "weaknesses" stem from our own lack of action. For example, the number of engineers significantly involved in community leadership or holding elected public office seems considerably inadequate.

Not only were there but three registered P.E.s in the U.S. Congress in 1996, there were less than three dozen registered P.E.s holding elected office in state legislatures throughout this entire country — 35 out of approximately 6000 seats (see Chapter 6). Not exactly a crowd.

And there doesn't seem to be much of a ground swell to change these numbers. I don't think the lawyers are "shaking in their boots" and worried about us taking decision-making positions away from them.

The future holds some real challenges for engineers — there are some major forks in the road for us.

So now, it is time to take the advice of the great sage of this book, Yogi Berra. It's time to take some of the forks in the road.

WHICH WAY?

Okay, but which forks, which directions?

We can continue to be technical advisors — advisors to decision-makers, to others who are leaders. Or we can move into decision-making positions ourselves — into policy leadership, a step or two above being an advisor.

Oh, there is nothing wrong with making things run, or in being a technical advisor; it is certainly better than not doing anything. At least you often get paid for being an advisor or a consultant, and do help to fulfill someone else's vision.

And, of course, not everyone wants to be — or should be — a leader. Why, even in the law profession, not every lawyer is a leader, not every lawyer holds a public office or is in the U.S. Congress, thank Heaven!

But in this rapidly emerging world so dependent on technology, if we could double or triple the number of engineers in leadership — if we could increase the number of P.E.s in state legislatures from three dozen to, say, a modest 100 — wouldn't that be significant?! Wouldn't that make a difference in how certain policy decisions are made? Wouldn't that influence the future direction of this country and the world?

Consider Bill Ratliff, a consulting engineer who has been a Texas state senator for eight years. He said, "It is amazing how much needed, in government, are the problem-solving skills of engineers. And not just on technical issues. Engineering skills and logic are needed for decisions on budgeting, investment, determining future goals — even on issues like education."

The world is run by those who show-up. Ratliff validates this. His experience proves, he noted, that "engineers can motivate change. All we need to do is show up." Ratliff is a shining example of truth in the old adage: one person can make a difference. (See Chapter Six.)

HONESTY POLICY

Among the real, true and basic strengths of our profession, three stand out:

1. Our skill — our technical expertise
2. Our ability to do something that adds value
3. Our honesty

This last point, honesty, is probably most important because of what it means for the other two. It is an honesty founded on the principle that we are trained to make decisions and arrive at solutions based on sound reasoning and science. We don't modify facts or alter numbers — change the value of gravity, for instance — just to make our answers come out right. No, we get the right answers, the honest answers.

What a potential for power and impact we would have if only we augmented — leveraged, if you will — these strengths with two other things. If we committed to:

- Become leaders in setting public policy.
- Broaden our outreach to the general public.

These two actions, not necessarily mutually exclusive, can each lead to the other. But if we just showed up more often — and in more places — our outreach would grow into leadership. Our leadership would bring a greater understanding of what we do and the significance of engineering in the economic and social advancement of our communities, our country and our world.

We engineers tend to keep to ourselves, talk only amongst ourselves, and stay ensconced in the ivory tower of our immediate colleagues and professional associations. But to make a real impact and get involved in the important work of setting public direction, we need to also talk and interface with people outside our industry.

In this way, we can successfully let the public know, for instance, how significant engineering was in accomplishing the Moon Landing and the Interstate Highway System. And, indeed, how significant it is now and will be in the challenges ahead on issues like housing, transportation, education, sustainable resources and quality of life.

LEADERSHIP INVOLVEMENT

To be a leader outside our industry — to help set public policy and direction — requires visibilty, involvement and commitment. (The first of these was dealt with in the previous chapter; the latter is a personal thing we must, each individually, grapple with.) Let us delve into involvement. Here are five things to consider doing. You don't have to do them all; just doing one or two would sway decisions. Remember, just showing up is an important first step.

1. Get involved in politics.
2. Serve on public boards and commissions.
3. Speak out — write and lecture.
4. Join and be active on issue-driven coalitions.
5. Support your professional engineering groups — work to enhance their political and public policy initiatives.

Let us take a closer look at each action item.

1. Get Involved in Politics

It is not necessary to be the governor of your state to change things, though that would be great. You do not even have to hold elective office to be effective and impact policy. (Chapter Six reflects on engineers as elected officials in some detail.) If you have no desire to run for public office, then support worthy candidates. Help get them elected, and let them know where you stand while you are doing it. Advise them about issues important to you which they may not be aware of or know about.

Once they are elected — if you are on a first-name basis — they will not only remember you and your issues, they will listen to your concerns on legislation they are debating, or indeed on legislation they propose. They will also introduce you — and your ideas and solutions — to other legislators, council members and policy makers. Now you've gone beyond showing up; you've become influential. You can now make a difference.

I will give you a real-life example. In Colorado, we fortunately have one of the 35 professional engineers in state legislatures (nationwide). But our guy, Senator Tom Norton from Greeley, who still owns his own consulting engineering firm in that Northern Colorado city, doesn't just serve in the Colorado Legislature; he has been the president of the Colorado Senate since 1993.

Senator Norton did not, of course, begin his political life as senate president, or even as an elected official. He began by being a consultant to municipalities, helping city officials grasp the technical and political aspects of public works. This led him to getting personally involved in local Republican party politics, first as a supporter of other candidates, and then as a candidate himself, in 1986, for a seat in the Colorado House of Representatives. Norton decided to run, he said, because as an engineer he was frustrated by state government agencies. He decided he would have a greater impact by going to Denver and becoming personally involved.

"It is critically important for engineers to be involved in politics at the day-to-day grassroots level in our communities," says Norton, whether it's serving on a school board, sewer board, planning commission, or city council. Local political involvement can help engineers strengthen their interpersonal skills, move their issues to the forefront, and formulate public policy. "Interpersonal skills, which are often difficult for engineers, are just as critical as problem-solving skills," he adds. Because of his grooming in local and regional politics, Norton feels he was well prepared to develop and advance far-reaching state policies once he was elected. "I believe that an engineer's everyday skills and methods of solving problems can easily, and quite successfully, be adapted to public service," he says.

Being able to actuate legislation and policies is often just a phone call away. Wayne Allard, the freshman U.S. Senator from Colorado, says on many important issues he — and he is not alone — only hears from a few of his constituents. Sometimes he receives only five or six letters or phone calls. If four of those favor a certain vote, he is influenced by that. So keep those "cards and letters" flowing to your elected officials. It does have an impact.

And again, you don't have to become the president of your state Senate or the governor of your state. Just showing up and getting involved means you will have an impact. And my next example on the action-item list, show good places to start.

2. Serve on Public Boards and Commissions

We can get involved with countless policy-making/policy-setting boards and commissions at the local, state and even national levels. In my state alone, we have more than 2,500 such important positions — just at the state level.

We are missing a golden opportunity when we don't show up, serve and participate on these types of bodies. They are where countless ideas — big and small ones — affecting policies and laws often germinate. Many times, they result in rules affecting our daily lives. Significant boards we can serve on include: long-range planning commissions, capital investment committees, economic development boards or construction safety commissions.

You can find out what's available by checking with your county and city clerks, mayor's office, city or town council staff, governor's office, leadership in your state senates and houses. And do not forget to check with members of your U.S. Congressional delegations.

These positions don't necessarily require a certain expertise or political party involvement, but they never hurt. Most people who serve on these boards are usually activists or have expressed a strong interest in getting involved — and got the attention of whoever makes appointments to a certain board or commission.

My appointment to the Historic Preservation Board, for instance, came about because I was close friends with the executive director of the State Historic Society. She recommended me and convinced the governor to appoint me, even though he and I are of different political persuasions. My state senator got me named to the state's Long-Range Planning Subcommittee in a similar way. There are other ways too — just presenting your credentials may work in your state or with your local agencies. What is important is: just do it.

By the way, if you don't want to be in leadership on a board or commission, you can still participate — and have some input to decisions — by serving on its advisory group. Many of these decision-making bodies have advisory groups who play important roles.

3. Speak Out — Write for General Readership Publications

Some ideas for writing and speaking out were covered in general in Chapter Four, but it is critically important to reiterate these points in the area of public policy. What is decided by policy-making bodies such as boards is often spurred on by public opinion. So if engineers are going to get involved in policy making, we must also get involved in shaping public opinion. The pen — and often times its cousin the podium — is mightier than the sword.

We can humanize and demystify engineering by writing and speaking out, but I caution that such presentations must always be made understandable to the average person-on-the-street. You can't lull them to sleep with too much technical engineering. But I know from experience that many groups and audiences are very interested in what an engineer has to say.

You can join Toastmasters or other public speakers groups — the National Speakers Association or its state-level chapters — to initiate speaking engagements to spread the word about your concerns. An enormous variety of groups — service clubs (Lions, Rotary, Optimists, etc.), other professional organizations like medical societies, community groups such as retired persons groups, chambers of commerce, etc. always seek good speakers, knowledgeable about construction or public works improvements going on (or being planned).

Talk to them about how an investment in infrastructure — that new bridge or highway or treatment plant — is an investment for future generations. Advocate a position on an issue of local or national concern. Sometimes groups like this just like hearing about "the engineering life" — the trials and tribulations of being an engineer — because our work is so "foreign" to them and "normal" life.

All kinds of local, state, regional and even national publications will accept guest columns or even regular feature or contributions. The media are always particularly interested in having people address the hot public debate topics of the time.

You may want to approach the largest newspaper in your city about writing a monthly column. If it is not interested, try a smaller paper or one of the many weekly or monthly local publications in your area.

I spent a great deal of time writing a regular column in Denver's leading business magazine on leadership — not on engineering but on leadership. I worked with and interviewed the movers and shakers in my area, got their ideas on the issues and saw things from their perspective. I shared them with a general business audience. Many of the leaders I interviewed and wrote about have major input on public policy and direction. I was, of course, always identified as a professional engineer. We always tried to discuss the hot topics of public interest at the time and, because of the high profile of many of my subjects, we lent something to the public discourse on important issues facing our region and the country.

4. Be Active on Issues-Driven Coalitions

Many coalitions — sometimes formed permanently in response to a major problem or temporarily in response to a burning but fleeting issue — offer wonderful opportunities to have a significant impact, meet a broad cross-section of people and, of course, get engineers involved. MADD (Mothers Against Drunk Drivers), tax reform and political term limitations coalitions are examples.

Many times legislation inspired by these groups affects our personal lives and the well-being of our communities. Often the new laws directly impact our businesses and profession.

For instance, in Colorado a few years ago — as in many other states — the cost and availability of liability insurance was at a crisis level and tort reform became a burning local issue. Individual engineers got involved, and led the group pushing for reform. It was a magic time in history. They headed up a coalition that included other like-minded professionals such as doctors, accountants, contractors and day-care providers. They succeeded in enacting tort reform legislation that has since served as a model for tort law reform nationally.

5. Support Your Engineering Societies

Actively support — with your time and money, with your ideas and wisdom — any professional and engineering groups that constantly lobby on our behalf, that advocate positions we believe in and are good for our profession, the public and our country.

Always keep in mind what that great American Teddy Roosevelt said: "Every man owes a part of his time and money to the business or industry in which he is engaged. No man has a moral right to withhold his support from an organization that is striving to improve conditions within his sphere."

Consider your own favorite organization (or organizations) for a moment. What can you do to strengthen or better support it in its efforts to improve the engineer's lot? Most long-standing engineering groups participate in worthy causes such as "Rebuild America", the private/public sector coalition (based in Washington, D.C.), currently serving as the watchdog for this nation's infrastructure. The more you can get involved with professional societies and other active associations within your specialty, the better for the profession as a whole.

Fundamental to the success of Rebuild America's efforts, for instance, will be that the U.S. Trust Funds (collected for transportation improvements) are released and used for the purposes for which they were collected. They were never meant to be used as budget-balancing mechanisms as is now being done.

Engineers can do much in the way of correcting this trickery by getting the public behind movements to encourage the president and U.S. Congress to use the monies for the badly needed improvements for which they were intended. This is but one of the many affairs we engineers and our organizations must get involved in to help build a better society — not only for us but for future generations.

On key, core issues, we must do what we can to get our favorite organizations to cooperate with and support the efforts of other like-minded engineering groups. As voiced by Charles Alexander (the 1997 president of IEEE*), "The true strength of the entire global engineering and scientific community and the depth of its persuasiveness rests in its ability to speak with 'one voice'." Two issues he feels this "one voice" can powerfully advance are: "the personal technical literacy of society as a whole" and "the importance of research and development for the betterment of our global society in the coming millennium."

HELP RUN THE WORLD

If more and more engineers take on leadership roles outside our industry — if more and more engineers show up at the top of society's "food chain" of decision makers — society will truly benefit. The world, so dependent on technology and engineering prowess, will surely be better served as well.

And we engineers can better impact policy decisions and the future. More and more often, we will be called upon not just to make things run, but to run things.

I urge you all, as strongly as I can, to get involved — not only in being leaders in this industry, in your companies or agencies, but also in your communities and in society.

There are so many opportunities for engineers — challenges we are more than capable of meeting — to set policy, to constructively impact and contribute, that I, for one, am truly enthusiastic. I am convinced that the greatness of engineering is set for even grander heights.

Now it's up to you. Seize the moment — show up and help run the world.

(*Footnote: IEEE = Institute of Electrical and Electronics Engineers, Inc.)

6

ENGINEERS AS LAWMAKERS

"Politics is too serious a matter to be left to the politicians."
—Charles de Gaulle

Engineers can no longer afford to sit passively on the sidelines while others shape public policy and our physical environment. The world has become too technologically complicated not to have some of those qualified to understand it — by virtue of their education, training and experience — at the table when debating the implications of scientific issues on political decisions.

The most effective way to have a hand in such debate, and in shaping political policy and setting public direction, is to hold elected public office — or appointed office. Getting so involved in government will enable us to be leaders in addressing critical quality-of-life issues now facing American communities. They include crumbling infrastructure, environmental decline, hazardous waste, public transportation, crime, health care and education — with many in our country functionally illiterate in science and technology.

Even though engineers have always been well qualified to apply innovative problem-solving skills in the public arena, our past track record at holding elected (or appointed) offices is dismal. Professional engineers are licensed to protect the public welfare, health, and safety while delivering the highest quality engineering solutions possible. Yet, while engineers are known to be behind making projects technically successful, we don't play a visible role in setting the policies that impact their use. Others — politicians, bureaucrats, lawyers, and business and community leaders, nearly all non-engineers — usually call the shots in policy decisions that impact public works projects and legislation governing the same.

Now more than ever, America needs greater numbers of producers knowledgeable about technology in public leadership positions to repair our infrastructure, revive our communities, protect our environment and keep us strong in today's competitive, global economy. It's time for engineers — as individuals and as a profession — to marshal their political leadership skills, show up and get involved, the more the better.

To date only a handful of America's estimated 2.5 million engineers have "shown up" on Capitol Hill or in our state houses. Fewer than one dozen have engineering degrees — only three that are registered professional engineers (P.E.s) — among the members of the 104th U.S. Congress, and only 35 P.E.s sat in the 6,000 seats of state legislatures in 1995. Nearly 70 percent of the members of U.S. Congress are lawyers because they tend to be in the right spots for government slots. They are trained as persuasive debaters and freely inject legislation with legalese — not necessarily logic or common sense — when they arrive on Capitol Hill and at state legislatures.

POLITICAL TRAINING SCHOOLS

According to a breakdown of state legislator occupants by the National Conference of State Legislatures, trends actually show a decrease in attorneys: from 22.3 percent in 1976 to 16.4 percent in 1986 to 15.7 percent in 1995. The survey also reveals a slight increase in legislators listed as engineers/architects/scientists — from 1.0 percent in 1976 to 1.4 percent in 1995. A good sign? I think so. Any increase — even a small one from 60 to 84 — in state legislators knowledgeable about the technical sciences, can only be a move in the right direction for getting better balanced government policy nationwide.

Medical doctors, it seems, are getting serious about holding elected, public offices. The American Medical Association (AMA) now has a candidate school in Washington, D.C. to train doctors for politics.

Nancy Warren, the AMA's director of political education, says doctors (and I'm sure the same can be said for engineers) examining political careers soon realize how different politics can be. "They are scientists accustomed to dealing with prescriptions and precise information putting issues into black and white categories." Though many political strategists feel doctors may be seen as too narrowly focused (does this sound familiar?), Dan Leonard of the national Republican Congressional Committee says, "We find that doctors have a lot of appeal and credibility with voters."

The same can be said about engineers. We have a lot a credibility — and voter appeal. Many of us, if we took the time, could get elected (or appointed) and hold public office. Not all of us want to, of course, but more of us *need* to if we are to truly have a significant role in shaping the future. Tomorrow's America (and the rest of the world) requires that more and more of its political leaders be highly familiar with modern-day technology, and able to use logic when debating, legislating and enacting the laws of the land. Some of those best equipped to lead the way — engineers — still remain in short supply.

In this chapter, we give the spotlight to a few engineer-lawmakers at national and state levels who have answered the call. They are now in the public arena leading America into the next millennium — and doing their part to energize and empower our profession. We will look into, not only *how* and *why* they got to where they are, but *if* engineers can be effective in elected public office. We salute these lawmakers for their commitment to service. Their dedication and accomplishments warrant our recognition and, as General Hatch suggests (in Chapter One): They are those engineers "we must celebrate" because, as "broader citizens," they are engaged "in public discourse."

NATIONAL PLAYERS

The only registered professional engineers currently serving in the 1996-8 U.S. Congress are in the House of Representatives: Joe Barton (R-TX), a consulting engineer from Ennis; John Hostettler (R-IN), a mechanical engineer from Wadesville; Jay Kim (R-CA), a civil engineer and former mayor of Diamond Bar.

"Every day, we benefit from the work of engineers," says six-term Rep. Barton. "Engineers are trained to find solutions to problems — a true benefit to my role as chairman of the House Commerce Subcommittee on Oversight and Investigations. This experience is invaluable." Barton also serves on the Science Committee where he championed the supercollider-superconductor project and NASA's space station. (Say what you will about the supercollider-superconductor, now on indefinite hold; it would have been a tremendous scientific asset for this country had it gone ahead.)

A former engineering consultant for Atlantic Richfield, Barton first ran for the House in 1984 to represent Texas' 6th district (suburban Dallas). In the debate over the 1990 Clean Air Act, he voiced Texas' concerns and successfully pushed an amendment requiring some cities to use portable pollution devices. In 1993, Barton sought (but did not get) the GOP nomination for the U.S. Senate where he would have been the only engineer.

Elected in 1994, Rep. Hostettler said his professional experience will shape his political life. The Republican adds that engineers believe there is one answer to a problem and that, as a Congressman, he will work hard to find that one answer to policy questions. His background has been helpful, he says, because engineers and scientists understand natural law — that "something is or isn't," he contends. "Engineers follow a rigid process to get the right facts, then use scientific methods to solve problems. When we look at problems in society, we can determine the right course to take."

In 1992, Rep. Kim became the first Korean-born American elected to Congress. As a member of the House Transportation and Infrastructure Committee, he has personal experience with the kinds of projects he oversees: repairing highways, bridges and waterways. His extensive engineering background makes it easier to listen to and understand testimony, analyze problems methodically and logically, and grasp statistics and numbers. "My constituents want to hear specific statistics or percentages rather than 'many, many'," he says.

In his goal to push for rebuilding America's deteriorating infrastructure, Kim says his biggest challenge is "getting other Congressmen to think like engineers." He expresses concern that logic doesn't always apply in politics. "As engineers with tunnel vision, we are trained to achieve results based on a set formula. We are taught that 1-plus-1 equals 2," he adds. "But here, 1-plus-1 can equal anything politicians want. There's a lot of compromising in Congress." As engineers," Kim stresses, "we don't compromise public safety for anything."

ENGINEERING STATE POLITICS

At state houses all across this land — in places like Denver, Topeka, Trenton, Austin and Phoenix — engineers are using their technical and political expertise to reinvigorate their communities, their state economies and their profession. These engineer-legislators have risen to leadership positions where they can influence the public and their colleagues. They generate better-informed decisions on initiatives needing engineering input and scientific background.

"If you want to hold public office, you don't have to start at the top," says Colorado State Sen. Tom Norton. Sen. Norton, who continues to run his own consulting engineering firm, worked his way up to the most powerful position in the state senate in a fairly roundabout way. He has served as its president since 1993. Norton embarked on his political path as a consultant helping local municipalities grasp the politics of public works. After spending time in local Republican party politics, he joined the Colorado House of Representatives in 1986. Norton ran because, as an engineer, he was frustrated with state government agencies; he decided it was easier to get things done by becoming personally involved in the government process.

Norton used his engineering problem-solving skills recently, as chair of the Senate Capital Development Committee, to get a much needed $100 million allocated for improving his state's infrastructure. He has also sponsored bills on such diverse subjects as workers' compensation laws, prison reform and construction. He has served on panels addressing telecommunications education for schools. Clearly, he does not fit the mold that engineers have tunnel vision. He has thrown his hat in the ring to run for governor of Colorado in 1998. If elected, he will be only one of two professional engineers holding such an office in the U.S., the other being Gov. Kirk Fordice of Mississippi.

In 1996, Kansas had more professional engineers (P.E.s) — four —in their legislature than any state in the Union. The most seasoned of the group of four, Sen. August "Gus" Bogina, Jr. of Shawnee was one of the state's most influential legislators for years. He retired after serving 21 years. The 67-year-old Republican chaired the upper chamber's powerful Ways and Means Committee for 11 years. But his days in public service aren't over: upon his retirement from the senate, Gov. Bill Graves appointed Bogina to chair the Kansas Board of Tax Appeals. "It's a new challenge and a new task," Bogina says. "It's also a way to change my focus, and I believe I can make a difference."

Making a difference is what inspires many citizens to get involved in public service. However, twenty-some years ago, Bogina recalls, "I had no delusions or thoughts that I could change state government. It was a matter of necessity that I got involved." Bogina ran for office in the lower house in 1974, he explains, because "the incumbent wasn't doing a good job. As a matter of fact, the incumbent came in third in the election."

Bogina stresses his background as a consulting engineer has paid off in government. He often tells young engineers: "We are problem-solvers by education and training, and problem-solvers have a place in government." His expertise with numbers, based on his engineering experience, has enabled him to better manage the state's $7.7 billion annual budget. As the state's spending watchdog, Bogina makes sure there's no red ink in Kansas.

"This job has required diplomacy and the ability to debate," Bogina says. The outgoing and persuasive engineer-politician jests he was once considered "the least likely to become an extrovert." In more serious accolade, Bogina built a reputation as "a tough guardian of the state treasury" and was recognized for it by the *Associated Press*.

The president of the consulting engineering firm Bogina, Hawley & Urkevich, Inc. admits a downside to his career in public service. He says, "It was necessary to make sacrifices to my practice. We had to weather some tough times," he observes, adding that certain potential clients, "wouldn't touch me because of my political status or affiliation."

New Jersey has General Assembly Speaker Garabed "Chuck" Haytaian, a former electrical engineer from Hackettstown. He reports that he applies his engineering training each day in leading his 80 house colleagues, including four fellow Republicans with engineering degrees. Among the four are: the assembly's deputy speaker, retired electrical engineer Nick Felice of Fair Lawn; aeronautical engineer Paul DiGaetano of Passaic, chair of the prestigious Policy and Rules Committee; chemical engineer Arthur Albohn of Morris County, head of the Solid and Hazardous Waste Committee; mechanical engineer Jack Gibson of Cape May County, who serves as vice-chair of Albohn's committee.

Legislators who think like engineers certainly make the speaker's job easier. "As elected officials, engineers follow a logical process in their deliberations to reach the bottom line and produce solutions," Haytaian explains. "When it comes to consensus building, no one can match the ability of engineers.

"One of the criticisms I hear," adds Haytaian, "is that engineers are not socially oriented, that we keep to ourselves. Well, that's not true here. Engineers in the assembly are very outgoing and personable. If we get involved in politics, we cannot be loners." Haytaian, who started his public service on a local school board, ran for the U.S. Senate in 1994. (Will he try again?)

Texas State Sen. Bill Ratliff, a former president of the American Consulting Engineers Council (ACEC) and a consulting civil engineer from Mount Pleasant, acknowledges his problem-solving skills are the most important qualities he brings to Austin. First elected in 1989, the Republican lawmaker says that "engineering is a method of solving problems — we take problems and chop them up into smaller components." His professional training helps him diagnose and resolve problems logically, using his engineer's mind to achieve results positive and universal.

"Bill sees things with an engineer's clarity," a Democrat colleague said. After another senator asked him a difficult question, Ratliff gave a logical answer. "Well, I really didn't want logic," joked his colleague. "When I first came to the Senate, I had to get over the notions that logic plays an important part in the political process," recalls Ratliff, echoing U.S. Rep. Kim's concern.

Like his Republican peer in Kansas, Ratliff uses his engineering thought process to trim red ink. He currently serves on the Senate Finance Committee (that oversees the state's $40 billion annual budget), the Legislative Budget Board and the Senate Committee on Natural Resources.

As chairman of the Senate Education Committee, Ratliff rewrote the state's educational code to make it a logically organized document for the first time. "Now," he says, "lay persons can find what they're looking for."

Since he is the only professional engineer in the Texas legislature, Ratliff's colleagues rely on him to grasp the significance of everyday technical and environmental issues. "Other legislators don't understand our world," he observes.

During his tenure, Ratliff has had to use common sense,

his knowledge of value-engineering and diplomacy to stop passage of four bills. They would have eliminated the state's version of the federal government's Brooks Bill which dictates that architects and engineers be selected for government contracts based on qualifications — QBS — and not low-ball bidding. In all four cases, the sponsors agreed to amend their legislation after Ratliff explained the impact the ill-fated bills would have on the quality of public works projects.

"Every solution that he proposes has structural integrity, whether he's advocating a bipartisan ethics commission, special rules for an East Texas oil field or a statewide approach to controlling hazardous waste," according to *Texas Monthly*, which twice has named Ratliff one of the state's best legislators. *The Dallas Morning News* hailed Ratliff as one of Texas' three best senators, citing his leadership in spearheading "a forward-looking education code."

"It's important for engineers to play a larger role in the political process," concludes Ratliff. He was inspired to enter politics after heading ACEC in the early 1980s, when he was deeply involved in federal and state legislative matters.

Phoenix consulting civil engineer David Eberhart, Majority Whip of the Arizona House of Representatives, got involved because of his interest in politics and commitment to community service. His activism began as a volunteer for charitable fund raisers, as a member of his local chamber of commerce and as a participant in his church's outreach efforts. "There's nothing more that we can give back to our communities than to serve the public," he points out.

"As problem-solvers who think logically, engineers bring a breath of fresh air to state legislatures," explains Rep. Eberhart. The three-term Republican, a former member of the Arizona State Board of Technical Registration, notes that many uninformed decisions are made by legislators not trained to tackle complex technical, environmental, and natural resource issues. "Lay persons often are overwhelmed by the technical side of issues and can be run roughshod over by lobbyists and special interest groups," he adds. "It is important for engineers who understand technical issues to assist public policy in the problem-solving area — and also to demonstrate to the public that engineering is truly a profession, not just a technical trade.

"We can elevate engineering in the eyes of the public by learning about and speaking out on public policy issues, by being involved in the legislative process and the community as a whole," Eberhart states. He urges each engineer to be more visible and involved in community activities. "By getting involved in politics, engineers can adjust the balance of the lawmaking machine to enact legislation that better serves the interests of our profession and society. To paraphrase one of ACEC's recent president's, Richard Weingardt: 'America needs our talent and leadership now. If we don't become part of our community's fiber, we're shirking our larger responsibilities'."

VOLUNTEERISM

A man who has never shirked his community duties — someone who personifies the type of volunteerism President Kennedy inspired with his "ask what you can do for your country" speech — is John Alger from Rumney, New Hampshire. David Siegel of *Engineering Times* reports that Alger, a professional engineer who ended a 38-year career with General Electric in 1988, can best be described as "a civic-minded whirlwind of volunteerism." Among other things, he serves as Rumney's town moderator and school moderator. A member of the conservation commission and the town planning board, he is also president of the Loon Lake Preservation Association.

In 1996 Alger was elected to the state House of Representatives from the 9th district, Grafton County. Asked why in his retirement he wasn't just taking it easy, relaxing and traveling, he replied, "You have to do something. You feel guilty if you're not doing something that makes the world better." About his civic activities, he allowed that he had lived a good life and felt he had something to contribute, "so why not do it. What else better is there to do with your money and time?"

Derek Owen, who serves with Alger on the state legislature's Environment and Agricultural Committee, is impressed with his thoroughness and how well prepared he always is. "He comes through as having given his questions considerable thought and having some good background." Would you expect anything less of an engineer-lawmaker having Alger's commitment to honor, duty and the betterment of society?

FIRE IN THE BELLY

The above engineer-lawmakers have gone the extra mile, offering their expertise and vision for the common good. As elected officials, their involvement is much more than simply responding to challenges mapped out by others. They sit at the table where the public agenda is being resolved and decisions are being made, and they offer their perspective — an engineer's — on what is best for society. We should celebrate them and their efforts; and even more than that, we should consider them role models. How many more from our ranks will emulate and join them?

Not that many of us need to hold elected federal or state public office to make a major impact, but certainly more than do now are needed. And more engineers are needed, as well, in elected local positions: city mayors, city council persons and county commissioners. That very well may be where our future senators, congressmen and congresswomen get their start — where, as political advisors say, "the fire in the belly" needed to run for political office gets lit. Our first political "fires" might even start at the neighborhood grassroots level, serving on school, planning, and community boards and commissions.

More engineers, not fewer, need to be proactive in tackling critical issues and serving in public leadership roles, if we are to control our own destinies and chart a brighter future.

How can engineering societies and professional associations help engineers become political leaders? We can borrow a page from the AMA and what doctors are doing: set up political training schools to help engineers learn about and understand the political process — learn how to get elected (and still keep our integrity!).

During 1995-6, ACEC commissioned four special blue-ribbon panels to study four critical areas, "four I's" — Imagination, Involvement, Information, and Impact. Our Impact panel, in particular, deliberated on ways to encourage busy professionals to participate in the world outside engineering, to climb the leadership ladder from our local communities to our state houses and U.S. Congress, and to prepare the next generation of engineers to become tomorrow's leaders — inside and outside our industry. The "four I's" initiative, which resulted in the publication of the ACEC book, *Seeing Into the Future (The I-Book)*, reaffirmed that today's engineers can *and must* leave their profession and society with a rich legacy of public leadership — a strong springboard from which to build a better world.

7

APOLLO 13 &
INFRASTRUCTURE

"The time to repair the roof is when the sun is shining."
—John F. Kennedy

Space travel, once the fantasy of dreamers and fiction writers, had already become routine when the crew of Apollo 13 blasted off in April 1970. Nine months after the world had celebrated the technological achievement of placing humans on the moon, three astronauts were once again making what some felt was a superfluous trip to collect more rocks.

HOLLYWOOD'S APOLLO 13

But as Ron Howard's award-winning movie "Apollo 13" showed, space travel was anything but routine. When an explosion crippled the spacecraft on the way to the moon, engineers and technical experts — many of whom had spent years developing the complex systems for the mission — found themselves with but a few hours to avert a fatal catastrophe 200,000 miles away.

Thanks to their resourcefulness, ingenuity, and gritty determination of the crew (and engineers at NASA's ground control center), Apollo 13 returned safely to earth. And less than a year later, Americans were once again walking on the moon.

A similar situation developed in the summer of 1997 with the damaged Russian MIR space station, which had an American astronaut aboard. Though the problem was dire and frustrating, ironically the Apollo 13 memory, spurred on by the recent movie, may have contributed to a general public nonchalance about MIR's plight.

Few would likely associate driving to the beach for a vacation or getting a drink of tap water with the complexities of space travel. Yet the same precision and innovation that went into designing moon rockets and space shuttles has helped create the infrastructure systems that are today part of our daily lives.

Half a century ago, who could have imagined we would be able to regularly transport millions of travelers and billions of dollars worth of commerce via a nationwide Interstate highway system; bring vast amounts of water to homes and communities, then return it safely to the environment; bring electrical power and other vital utilities to even the most isolated regions of our land.

As well-designed as the Apollo 13 spacecraft was, it was still subject to problems and glitches, one of which nearly proved fatal. Likewise, our superbly engineered transportation and utility systems cannot last forever.

DETERIORATING INFRASTRUCTURE

Beset by years of steadily increasing demands and shrinking improvement budgets, the safety of America's citizens is in jeopardy. Highways and bridges, many designed for 1950's traffic loads, can barely support today's transportation needs, let alone those of the next century. Some 2,000 of the country's four million miles of highways crumble and must be replaced each year. A bridge collapses every other day in America.

Washington's Woodrow Wilson Bridge — a crucial link on the East Coast's primary interstate highway — has literally worn out under the daily stress of more than 172,000 vehicles, at least double its original design capacity. Yet, no firm plan for replacing or improving the structure is in sight.

Hundreds of small, rural communities lack safe, efficient systems for treating sewage, while antiquated pipelines threaten thousands of urban dwellers with frequent service disruptions and contaminated drinking water. On average throughout this country, an estimated 15 gallons of water are lost for every 100 gallons consumed because of leaky pipes.

More than 10,000 dams in the U.S. are classified as high hazard. In 1995, on the same day that heavy rains and floodwaters devastated portions of several mid-Atlantic states, NBC's "Dateline" news show revealed that hundreds of dams across the nation are on the verge of failure. With ownership and maintenance responsibility for many of these facilities in doubt, we face a series of costly and potentially fatal incidents should the dams become stressed beyond their weakened limits.

What sets our infrastructure crisis apart from the Apollo 13 experience is the time to correct these problems before they become more serious. But time is of the essence. With estimates to merely *correct* existing deficiencies ranging into the hundreds of billions of dollars, we must act now to implement a long-term program to rebuild our infrastructures before they reach a point of no return.

Such a program cannot simply address short-term needs nor be limited by demographic and political concerns. We need to examine the entire spectrum of our infrastructure systems from the largest city to the most remote rural community, develop effective programs for improvement, and incorporate strategies for adapting and expanding these systems as needs change. The scope of this effort is enormous, but so are the consequences of inaction.

ALARMING STATISTICS

The following identifies some major concerns voiced by the Rebuild America Coalition (a broad coalition of public and private organizations committed to the infrastructure challenge):

• Airways are congested. Air traffic control needs substantial up-grading to maintain safety. (The Federal Aviation Authority - FAA - estimates that 58 airports will be "seriously congested" by year 2000, up from 16 in 1986. Congestion will affect 74% of passengers, compared with 39% in 1986%.)

• 31 percent of the country's public schools were built before World War II; another 43% were constructed in the 1950s and 1960s to accommodate the baby boom. National cost of deferred school repairs is estimated to be more than $100 billion.

• Water storage and distribution systems are deteriorating in older cities. Leaking pipes cause some to lose as much as 30% of their daily water supply. In a recent two-year period, 34 cities averaged 229 water main breaks per 1,000 miles of main.

• America will need more than 3,300 new wastewater treatment facilities by year 2012. (According to EPA, about 10,850 wastewater facilities have water quality or public health problems.)

• Despite a $44 billion federal investment in sewage treat-

ment since 1972, it will take $84 billion to meet the require-
ments of the Clean Water Act by 2005. More than 28 million
Americans are not served by modern sewage treatment facilities.

• The average age of transit buses now exceeds recommended usable age by 20 to 35% and 20-30% of rail transit facilities and maintenance yards are in poor condition (according to
the American Public Transit Association).

• About 35% of the Interstate system will have outlived
its useful life in 1995, and the cost of maintaining the system
could exceed the initial $120.5 billion cost of construction.

• In 1989, almost 70% of daily peak-hour travel on urban
Interstate systems occurred under congested conditions. By
2005, traffic delays caused by inadequate roads will cost the
nation $50 billion a year in lost wages and wasted gasoline.

• Some 265,000 miles of U.S. roads — 56% of major roadways — were rated as poor in 1990. About half of the country's highways are at or near the point where vehicle operations are impaired by deteriorating conditions.

• Total public spending on infrastructure is dropping significantly, from 3.6% of the Gross National Product (GNP) in
1960 to 2.6% in 1985. The relative share of public works spending at all levels of government declined from nearly 20% of
total expenditures in 1950 to less than 7% in 1984.

Dean Baker and Todd Schafer point out in *The Case for
Public Investment* (an Economic Policy Institute publication)
that the "public capital stock" — the "sum of the nation's existing public roads, bridges, water treatment plants and other
structures; the infrastructure on which the economy stands and
grows" — has fallen "without interruption, from nearly 55% of
gross domestic product (GDP) in 1982 to less than 40% in
1992." In dollar values, the public infrastructure of 1992 fell
roughly $1 trillion short of that of a decade earlier. When com-

pared with the G-7 nations — America's major economic competitors — the U.S. is at the bottom in infrastructure investment. In 1992, as an example, Japan's investment as a percentage of its GDP was three times that of the U.S. "This widening investment gap," say Baker and Schafer, "is bad news for America's ability to compete in the 21st century and to provide the kinds of jobs that can raise living standards."

USER CONCERNS

I suppose that, as an engineer often involved in bridge building and road design, I could be accused of a vested interest in making claims of poor and deteriorating infrastructure. Let me cite an authority representing the users, the president of the American Automobile Association (AAA), Robert Darbelnet.

In 1996, AAA teamed up with the Federal Highway Administration (FHWA) on a state-by-state study of the condition of the nation's road bridges. According to the study, every single state in the union — all 50 — had at least 10 percent of its bridges in deficient shape, with the leader being the state of New York where 63 percent of its 17,308 bridges were found to be either structurally deficient or functionally obsolete. The study found that, overall, 32 percent of the nation's 574,671 bridges were deficient, an appalling and potentially dangerous situation. (More on this later in this chapter).

"We have reached this era of decaying bridges, crumbling roadways and antiquated air traffic control because the government is investing only a fraction of what is needed for infrastructure maintenance," said AAA's Darbelnet in releasing the study. "The FHWA estimates it needs $53 billion a year just to maintain current road and bridge conditions, and $72 billion a year to make improvements. Current spending is only $35 billion — a virtual guarantee that the system will get worse. More inefficient. More dangerous."

CAN WE DO ANYTHING?

Can we change this picture? In his "Apollo 13" portrayal of astronaut Jim Lovell, Tom Hanks notes that it didn't take a miracle to put man on the moon, but that "we just decided to do it." America can't wait for a miracle to resolve its infrastructure crisis. Fortunately, just as the planned flight and emergency rescue of Apollo 13 were made possible, in large part, by skilled aerospace and computer engineers, America has the talents of its professional engineers to help rebuild the nation's infrastructure.

They can apply the same expertise that has continually improved our nation's quality of life into designing new systems — and restoring existing ones — that will serve society's changing needs well into the 21st century. And if an emergency occurs — whether it's a natural disaster, a toxic spill or even a terrorist attack — these same individuals will, as they always have done, be available. They will use their knowledge to protect the public from further harm, contain and correct the damage, and help expedite the process of recovery.

In today's world, however, America's engineers must take a more aggressive role in forwarding this exciting and much-needed initiative to the arenas of public debate. Solving the infrastructure problems on earth will require the same degree of teamwork that made Apollo 13 a triumph of courage and innovation rather than a tragedy. That teamwork will demand support from the average person-on-the-street to the highest levels of government.

Crucial will be a commitment from the leaders of government, business and industry to recognize the critical need for action and take the proper steps toward renewing our vital infrastructure systems. Engineers must find the ways to work together with these types of leaders, identifying innovative funding mechanisms that will prevent essential projects from languishing for lack of dollars. We must analyze emerging technologies that will improve both the operation and durability of these systems. And we must formulate a comprehensive implementation strategy that emphasizes quality rather than cutting corners for financial expediency.

It took only 66 years for America to go from the first powered flight to landing humans on the moon. Surely, the challenge of saving our critical infrastructure is no less achievable if we put our best resources to the task. In doing so, we engineers must not only use our technical abilities but our leadership skills as well to help implement a sound plan of rebuilding today, before our skills are needed to resolve an inexorable crisis tomorrow.

IN THE KNOW

In the winter of 1995-6, the American Consulting Engineers Council (ACEC) undertook a national survey of our members to ascertain their outlook for America. In it we found that the nation's engineers are bullish on America's economy for the remainder of the decade. But the majority feel this country's investment in upgrading and improving its infrastructure is either lacking or terrible.

As far as the future of our country's well-being is concerned, survey respondents sent a clear message: Congress and the president need to balance the federal budget, and ensure proper and reasonable funding for infrastructure. They must make a commitment not only to fiscal responsibility but also to the vast infrastructure systems that support our nation's economy.

Certainly many needs must be carefully considered in this process, but we as a nation cannot hope to achieve any of our goals without providing the resources for a sound infrastructure. This nation's economic well-being and everyone's standard-of-living depend on it.

In assessing the overall state-level outlook, the most optimistic responses came from the South and Midwest where respondents believe the on-going economic turnaround in their regions will lead to a better business climate. Elsewhere, most believed there will be little change over the next several years. A handful of respondents from the Rust Belt predict a slowdown due to their states' budget problems and a shrinking manufacturing base.

The survey also indicated civil, structural and environmental services will be in high demand, with the strongest markets being transportation, water/wastewater facilities, environment remediation and other infrastructure-related projects. Midwest and West respondents saw an upturn in residential and industrial development, while the Northeast will focus on rehabilitating their existing transportation networks. Many consulting engineers in the South think they will stay busy designing commercial and industrial projects over the next few years.

In assessing the most important state-level issues, engineers cited a wide range of concerns, most of which relate to encouraging or sustaining economic growth. Some listed state taxes, interest rates, and education as being key issues for the future, while others believed the shift of federal responsibilities to the states will have a significant impact on local economies and construction activity.

As at the national level, financing for state public-works projects was of particular concern. Nearly two-thirds agreed that state investments in upgrading and improving infrastructure are woefully inadequate.

As we consider this, to my way of thinking, nothing symbolizes better the beauty of engineering infrastructure, or pinpoints the crisis more, than bridges. They are highly visible — and they are points of national pride and honor for every country around the globe.

I find myself disheartened that, for many years now, the U.S. — the most powerful country in the world — does not have the bragging rights for building the longest-span suspension bridge. That record, currently held by Great Britain, will soon pass on to Denmark then Japan. (See table of suspension bridge record-holders.)

TABLE 7A

World's Longest-Span Bridges:
13 bridges with clear spans over 1,000 meters

Bridge, Location, Year Completed	Span in Meters
1. Akashi Kaikyo, Akashi Straits, Japan (1998)	1,990
2. Great Belt East Bridge, Denmark (1998)	1,624
3. Humber, Humber River, Britain (1981)	1,410
4. Verrazano Narrows, New York (1964)	1,298
5. Golden Gate, San Francisco Bay (1937)	1,280
6. Hoga Kusten, Angerman River, Sweden (1997)	1,210
7. Mackinac Straits, Michigan (1957)	1,158
8. Minami Bisan Seto, Inland Sea, Japan (1988)	1,100
9. Second Bosporus, Turkey (1992)	1,090
10. Ataturk, Bosporus, Turkey (1973)	1,074
11. George Washington, Hudson River, NY (1931)	1,067
12. Tejo, Lisbon, Portugal (1966)	1,013
13. Firth of Forth, Queensferry, Scotland (1964)	1,006

Notes:

1. Colorado's Royal Gorge Bridge (1929) is still the world record holder for vertical clearance — 321 meters.

2. Work is now underway on the Messina-Sicily Bridge (in Italy), which may be the longest ever.

THE BEAUTY OF BRIDGES

Fifty years ago when I was a young boy, my parents took our family on a vacation to the mountains — the Rocky Mountains. We lived on the high plains of northeastern Colorado then. On that particular trip I saw something that would affect me for the rest of my life. It both impressed and startled me; it helped me decide my career.

We visited the Royal Gorge, that deep canyon carved out of solid granite by the Arkansas River. There I saw the bridge: the stunning, glittery Royal Gorge suspension bridge. It was magnificent. It stretched out for a quarter of mile over a canyon as deep as it was wide. That is when I knew I was going to become a engineer and design structures.

Bridges are one of the most wondrous things man has ever built. They are designed to carry people, vehicles and materials over an infinite variety of both man-made and natural barriers. This singleness of purpose distinguishes them from other forms of structure. The design of building structures, for example, is concerned with people requirements: heating, ventilation, lighting and so on. Most of the time, the structure is not the dominant factor.

In a bridge, structure dominates and is exposed. Bridges are important because of their usefulness. To be sure, their visible appearance can be a vital aspect of their design and should not be discounted. But, at the root, bridges serve practical, utilitarian functions which is the essence of their existence. Among the most visible and important manifestations of civil engineering in our environment, bridges are essential components of our public works foundation, our most obvious example of infrastructure. Bridges become part of our landscape, both in beauty and function.

Since I first looked upon the Royal Gorge, I have traveled many places and seen many spectacular bridges — outstanding suspension bridges many times longer and larger than the Royal Gorge Bridge. But it was the first to make me think about structures; what they do for us; how and why they get built.

BEST OF THE BRIDGES

I am not alone in the engineering community in my affection for bridges and I believe the general public, too, is fascinated. Because of this, years ago I did a "Best Bridges" survey in my home state of Colorado — asking opinions of engineers, architects, bridge builders and public officials — and the response to it was overwhelming. The effort and the survey results received enormous media play in magazines and newspapers both within and outside the state. It was clear that just about everyone, engineer and layman alike, had strong opinions and great fondness for bridges.

A few years later, in late 1994, ACEC did a similar survey of "Best Bridges," this time looking nationally for opinions. This countrywide effort drew much attention as well. What follows is taken from my report of that survey.

Almost 600,000 bridges span gorges, rivers and other obstacles across the United States, ranging from small timber structures in rural areas to majestic, towering landmarks, such as the Golden Gate Bridge in San Francisco and the Brooklyn Bridge in New York. (Both were the world's longest-span suspension bridges when built: Brooklyn in 1883 and Golden Gate in 1937.) Some bridges carry as few as one vehicle a day — perhaps a lone tractor traveling between fields on a farm — or many thousands of vehicles a day, as does the Tappanzee Bridge connecting New Jersey to Upstate New York, the George Washington Bridge over the Hudson River (NY) or the San Francisco/Oakland Bay Bridge in California. (The Washington is the most heavily used bridge in the world, carrying 100 million vehicles per year.)

Bridges are perhaps the most critical components of our surface transportation network because they ensure the continuity of mobility. The chain is only as strong as its weakest link, and our roads and highways are only as sound as the bridges that connect them.

Bridges represent the "can do" spirit of America. "Each bridge is unique — reflecting use and topographical constraints as well as the talents of its design engineer and builder," said Les MacFarlane, president of ACEC at the time of the survey. Our bridges truly are national treasures.

For its survey, ACEC asked its members — the bridge experts themselves — what they consider to be the best bridges in America. Criteria they were asked to consider included innovation, challenge and uniqueness of design, sheer beauty, size and other characteristics that might make one particular bridge stand out from others.

Some bridges identified by ACEC members included the more spectacular bridges, such as the aforementioned Brooklyn Bridge and Golden Gate Bridge. Many, though, were smaller, less well-known but significant bridges that engineers felt were simply well-designed, interesting or innovative.

More than 200 great bridges were recommended for inclusion as America's "Best Bridges." Twelve were finally selected as being the best of the best. (They are listed in the accompaning table.) Comments on these fascinating structures ranged from "a miracle in engineering design and construction" to "one of the few great bridges that you can see and enjoy close up."

A member from Georgia included an excerpt from a letter-to-the-editor in *The Atlanta Journal-Constitution* describing one Atlantan's admiration of the futuristic Tom Moreland Interchange: "Every time I see its soaring curves filled with movement, and think about its usefulness and complexity, and all the human work and creativity that went into it, I get goose bumps... it's what great art should be."

TABLE 7B

America's 12 "Best Bridges"
As selected by ACEC Consulting Engineers
(ADT=Average Daily Traffic)

NAME *Location*	Year Built *ADT*	Construction Type
Brooklyn Bridge *New York City, NY*	1883 *110,500*	5,858-foot steel suspension
Wire Bridge *New Portland, MA*	1842 *500*	198-foot timber suspension
I-295/James River *Richmond, VA*	1990 *13,000*	4,686-foot concrete- stayed girder
Golden Gate Bridge *San Francisco, CA*	1937 *114,300*	9,000-foot suspension
Houston Ship Channel *Houston, TX*	1982 *18,000*	7,582-foot concrete
Glenwood Canyon *Glenwood Springs, CO*	1980-92 *12,000*	post-tensioned segmental concrete
Clark Bridge *Alton, IL*	1994 *16,000*	4,620-foot cable-stayed
Tom Moreland *Atlanta, GA*	1985 *181,000*	262-foot steel girder
Yaquina Bay Bridge *Newport, OR*	1934 *13,500*	3,223-foot steel arch
Father Louis Hennepin *Minneapolis, MN*	1855 *19,000*	1,040-foot steel suspension
Roosevelt Lake Bridge *Roosevelt, AZ*	1992 *900*	Steel arch bridge
Rainbow Bridge *Niagara Falls, NY*	1941 *10,000*	1,200-foot steel arch

No doubt there are many award-winning, or award-deserving, bridges across the American landscape that generate "goose bumps." The ACEC survey not only identified several great bridges, but it also called attention to the growing number of bridges that are not so attractive, many of which need repair or replacement because they are worn out.

More than 19,000 of America's bridges have been in service since the turn of the century, and another 163,737 are at least half a century old. Bridges built that long ago may have been designed to last at least 50 years, but were not expected to carry the high volumes of traffic they do today. Many show signs of wear and tear, and need to be rehabilitated or completely reconstructed.

FHWA reports that one in every three bridges is rated "functionally obsolete" or "structurally deficient" and in need of major improvements, and that nearly 200 bridges collapse or buckle every year. Inadequate design, poor construction and shabby maintenance are often a major cause of the problem. The 190,500 FHWA-identified, deficient bridges include small, short-span creek crossing bridges, large suspension bridges, Interstate bridges carrying thousands of vehicles daily, and others between these extremes.

An article titled "Day of Reckoning is Here" in *USA Today* (Aug. 29, 1994) reported that the problem is worst in the Northeast where more than half of the busiest bridges — those carrying more than 15,000 vehicles a day — are deficient. "In most cases, ailing bridges go unnoticed until they suffer severe damage from inattention and require expensive, traffic-jamming repairs," *USA Today* reported. "If a bridge is repaired, painted, resurfaced and maintained, it will last longer and require fewer major improvements than if it is neglected for years at a stretch. Preventive maintenance, it's called, or 'A stitch in time saves nine.'"

Until 1970, state and local governments had to shoulder all bridge improvements. And since it is generally less expensive (and frequently more politically palatable) to repave many miles of roadway rather than rebuild one expensive bridge, bridge rehabilitation has remained a lower priority.

In 1970, the federal government became involved following the collapse of the Silver Bridge in Ohio. Congress passed the Federal Aid Highway Act of 1970, establishing the "Special Bridge Replacement Program" (SBRP) to provide matching federal funds — generated through the federal motor-fuel tax — for bridge construction and reconstruction.

In the late 1970s, the SBRP evolved into the Highway Bridge Replacement and Rehabilitation Program which, through 1994, had obligated $45 billion to fund replacement or rehabilitation of some 87,000 bridges. This is less than half the number that need major repair or replacement.

The new Intermodal Surface Transportation Efficiency Act of 1991 (ISTEA) has authorized $16.1 billion in federal funding over six years for bridge rehabilitation. Although this is more than the allotments in previous years, it still is far less than what is needed.

QUALITY BRIDGE BUILDING

Because bridges are such a major public works investment and critical link in the transportation network, they must be designed and constructed using the highest standards. They must be efficient, economical, safe, aesthetic, low in maintenance, and built primarily for strength and long life to endure growing traffic, hostile weather and the natural wear and tear of age. Because of this, it is always wise to have bridges designed by engineering firms with proven expertise and skill.

To ensure the best design firms are chosen for the job, qualifications-based selection (QBS) procedures — selection based primarily on qualifications rather than low price alone

— has stood the test of time. The concept — labeled the Brooks Architectural and Engineering Act — was passed into federal law in 1972 to insure quality design and construction for federal projects and federally-funded public works projects at the local or state government levels.

"It is absurd for public agencies to select bridge designers by low bid — just as their purchasing agents buy typewriters, shovels or trucks," said Tom Norton, P.E., President of the Colorado State Senate. "It is an abdication of their responsibility to their public, which is to see that taxpayers get the most for their tax dollars. Value engineering suggests that it is misleading to save a few dollars on the least costly portion of bridge construction — design."

A review of bridge design entries in ACEC's prestigious Engineering Excellence Awards competition shows that roughly 90 percent of the finalist and award-winning projects typically are designed by firms that were selected through a QBS process.

"When the focus of a project is quality rather than strictly cost — from the beginning of the design phase to the end of construction — it's bound to be a winner in all ways: durability, innovation, aesthetics, and function," according to ACEC's MacFarlane. "The ultimate winner is, of course, the 'owner' of the bridge...the taxpayer who helped pay for it and who uses it daily."

It is important for Americans to stop, every so often, to appreciate the beauty and strength of bridges — those connections so vital to our transportation networks. Not all that long ago, people had to wade through streams or ford rivers, scale mountain canyons and navigate hilly terrain to get where they wanted to go. Many days were spent just trying to get from one side of the river or mountain to the other. But things have changed.

Now, unless a bridge falls down or is closed to traffic

because it might collapse, most people don't typically think about the tremendous impact these structures have on their daily lives.

Economists have noted for years the direct correlation between closed or weight-restricted bridges and the increased costs of products and raw materials that must be brought into towns over lengthy circuitous detours. Many local governments have realized the importance of solid, reliable transportation systems too late, when new businesses and industries choose not to locate in towns and cities where bridges are too weak to service the increased traffic of additional commerce.

ACEC's survey of America's "Best Bridges" was meant to bring attention to these works of grandeur designed by engineers, and it did. It also reminded us that decades of wear and tear have reaped their toll and left us with a backlog of serious bridge repair challenges.

INFRASTRUCTURE AT LARGE

As I mentioned earlier in this chapter, I have included this specific look at bridges because I think it neatly encapsulates the entire argument for investment in infrastructure. Along with our bridges, we see a deteriorating infrastructure crisis in many other areas: aging water and sewer systems, electrical power systems, roads and highways, local streets, airports, etc. Nearly every part of our nation's infrastructure must be tended to if we are to handle the ever-growing needs of our country.

When you consider the United States is among the most advanced countries on earth and we find ourselves in this situation, think about the plight of the rest of the nations. Many of them, especially in the developing nations of South America,

Africa, Asia and Eastern Europe, started with inferior infra-structure. They now face the dual problem of fixing what now exists while providing the new facilities that will ensure economic development.

We all have a stake in the assurance of economic vitality and development in the U.S. and throughout the world. Engineers will, by nature, be at the core of making this maintenance and development happen. They will not only ensure our own quality of life will be maintained, but also ensure the quality of life for the rest of the world will expand. The establishment of quality of life in the developing world will go a long way in helping the U.S. economy stay strong and grow. It will keep the rest of the world looking hopefully toward a future without war and catastrophe.

American engineers not only will play a key role in how all this develops, we must take a pro-active stance — take leadership — in making sure it happens properly. We owe it to ourselves as professionals to take a leading role. We owe it to our countrymen and the rest of the world to offer our expertise and creativity.

Without strong infrastructure, there is disorder and stagnation. This does not have to be, nor will it be the case, if we engineers get involved as the leaders we are capable of being, and champion the cause.

8

THE WEALTH CREATORS

"The reward of a thing well done, is to have done it."
—Ralph Waldo Emerson

Awe-inspiring space travel...instantaneous communications...labor saving robots...soaring bridges...towering skyscrapers...laser control systems...lifesaving heart pacemakers. All these have one thing in common: they were ideas that became reality thanks to engineers.

Yet for all these contributions toward building our modern world, many people don't know much about engineers and what they do. Some have even called engineering the "stealth profession," even though more than two million Americans are engineers.

NATIONAL ENGINEERS WEEK

Ever since 1951, when President Harry S. Truman proclaimed the first National Engineers Week, it has been observed each February during the week that begins with Presidents' Day because, as everyone knows (?), our first president was a surveyor and engineer. At this time, all through the halls of government and the corridors of political power, in the smoke-filled back rooms and at the tables of power-lunching is heard a great celebration of a noble profession that has made America the economic envy of the world.

Well, okay, maybe that's a bit strong. Yet, engineering has played an enormous role in the building of America and will continue to be a vital aspect of our future. It's just doubtful that there are ever any great public celebrations exalting engineers during their week. Certainly nothing approaches the Egyptian's exhalation of Imhotep, engineer of the pyramids, when they placed him on a level with their gods upon his death.

Typically, National Engineers Week, the time to reflect on the state of a most critical national asset, our engineering base and the men and women whose work is so vital to our "standard of living," comes and goes with little fanfare or public awareness.

And that's too bad because, as we debate the concern about America's ability to maintain its competitiveness — some suggest it is in serious decline in sectors like manufacturing — and look for ways to strengthen, rebuild and restore productivity, many answers to our problems will spring from the training and expertise found in engineering.

"Other countries — our competitors — glorify those who create designs and those in manufacturing because they see the linkage between productivity, world competitiveness and the viability of their societies," commented Jack Welch, CEO of General Electric Co., when he was honorary chair of National Engineers Week.

"What passes for conventional wisdom has decreed 'America is shifting out of manufacturing and into services.' But those who spend their days struggling to compete with the best competition the world offers, in both services and manufacturing, see clearly that a nation must have a viable manufacturing base if it is to develop and maintain a viable service base," he continued.

Welch added, "To whom is it left to see that American innovation is dynamic enough and American productivity growth sufficiently rapid to win in world markets? In large measure, it is the engineer and, in that context, America needs to see the profession as the bodyguard of its standard of living."

Former Colorado Governor Richard Lamm, a lawyer, adds to Welch's perspective, saying: "We should understand that wealth will flow to the nations that have the best wealth-creating teams. Scientists, engineers and technicians are wealth creators." He even suggests there is a correlation to a country's GNP (gross national product) — a key factor in its standard of living: the more engineers, the higher the GNP.

WEALTH CREATORS

They are wealth creators because they solve problems that lead to producing the basis of wealth. America became a world leader and economic power by setting high standards of invention and production. We created products the world needed, developed production techniques and built plants and equipment to deliver the goods. We designed and developed communications systems that literally changed the way business is conducted worldwide. And we designed and built a transportation system that made America the most mobile society in history.

None of these developments would have been possible without people trained in mathematics, science and technoogy — and engineers are at the core of such training. Future advances that maintain and elevate American productivity will require that the best and brightest are educated to tackle the ever-more-complex challenges inherent in modern technology, engineering and rapid change.

Unfortunately, we are producing a generation which, in this politically correct environment, can best be described as "technically challenged."

As far back as 1980, we became aware of the problem when a major study was released that showed American school children lagging far behind their peers in Japan and Taiwan in math and science skills. The "math gap" it was called. At the time, a hue and cry erupted; and politicians, educators and parents got together to attack the problem. But nothing happened. The original "math gap" researchers recently went back to the same schools tested a decade before to study current students. They also followed up with those originally tested and, in a new study published in *Science* magazine, found the same "math gap" still exists today.

No wonder we now look at the Japanese as the world model for productivity. What *is* surprising is that we consider this Japanese productivity the result of either some cultural difference or better business models that we could somehow artificially emulate.

The truth is Japan educates more engineers by far than we do, and elevates more of them to business and industry leadership. They place a greater emphasis in school *and* in the workplace on such pragmatic skills as mathematical, scientific and technological understanding. Ironically, many Japanese business models we so revere — the most important being Total Quality Management — were introduced to the Japanese after World War II by an American, W. Edwards Deming. Regrettably, his principles of management weren't exactly embraced by American business when unveiled in the late 1940s.

We need a new commitment to developing strong reasoning skills, both in our schools and in business, if we are going to keep a strong economic presence in the new world order. We are not just fighting the tigers of the Pacific Rim and places like Singapore; a big sleeping giant, China, will soon hit the scene.

During many of the national elections in the 1990s, debate focused on the need to halt the drain of American production jobs to cheaper labor markets overseas. The best way to accomplish this is to have problem-solvers, like engineers, attack productivity problems: to upgrade American plants and equipment, create new types of manufacturing and develop new products and industries. They would show expertise not just as technicians to deliver on wild ideas presented by dreamers, but in leadership roles where engineers can bring realistic creativity to bear.

DETERIORATION OF OUR BASE

But something disturbing appears to be happening to America's engineering base. Many of our trained, experienced engineers and technicians are aging and retiring. And our young people are increasingly opting for careers in other fields. Also, many senior, experienced engineers are getting out of engineering and taking higher paying or less demanding jobs. This decline of our American-born engineering expertise has ominous implications for our ability to continue to survive in the global marketplace — at least, in the upper echelon.

THE FUTURE DEPENDS ON OUR YOUTH

Perhaps part of our inability to appreciate analytical skills and technical professions comes from our national obsession with glamour and celebrity. Engineers and others of their ilk are thought of as unglamorous if, indeed, they are thought of at all. (How to deal with this issue was discussed in Chapter Four.)

At a time when our government struggles with such vital challenges as maintaining and growing American productivity, rebuilding American infrastructure and re-energizing American education, it is important to note the declines in each coincided with a de-emphasis on problem-solving skills and careers.

Private/public-sector partnerships must be established to work with educators as well as state and local governments to improve science, math and vocational education at all levels. Technical education must be elevated to a higher plane. Skilled technicians and craftsmen who work with their hands as well as their minds — carpenters, plumbers, mechanics, repairmen and the like — are required everywhere. Mechanical engineer George Wallace, P.E., a visionary and founder of the world famous Denver Technological Center, says a million or so of these types of jobs go unfilled each year in the U.S.

American engineers need to assert their leadership and heed the advice of Welch to, "roll up their sleeves and do again for the nation what they did a half a century ago: make (and keep) us a winner in the world marketplace" this year and next and in the future. We need to take the time and do what it takes to identify, encourage and recruit our best young men and women — our future stars — into careers that produce and build. We want to increase the size of the economic pie, not merely divide and redistribute the same old one over and over. We need to be steadily improving, not eroding, our living standards and quality of life.

WHAT CAN BE DONE?

National Engineers Week (NEW) each February is a good time to renew our commitment to produce the best the world has ever seen, recognize and celebrate the wonders engineering has produced, and become aware of new things we will create. We can use the general media and the proclamations from the president, members of Congress and famous business people who happen to be engineers, including Welch, Lee Iaccoca and Norm Augustine, to gain public awareness.

But more than this has to be done to make NEW a meaningful celebration. Like Ebenezer Scrooge at the end of Charles Dickens' *A Christmas Carol*, we need to figure out a way to celebrate this important season "all the days of the year."

Hopefully ideas put forth in this book will generate the spark to have engineers get more aggressive (as leaders?) in seeing their vision debated in public forums.

If we act now, in a proactive way, the predictions for an impending decline in the engineering, manufacturing and production base of this country will disappear.

Emerson told us that if we build a better mousetrap, the world would beat a path to our door. Americans are still the most creative people in the world. Let's go build those "better mousetraps."

NEW not only takes place around the birthday of President Washington, but also that of the inventor of one of the world's wonders of amusement, the Ferris Wheel. These towering attractions have amazed carnival-goers young and old alike, for more than 100 years. Its inventor? George Washington Gale Ferris, a civil engineer. Some say it's more than coincidence that it took an engineer to, not just build a "better mousetrap," but offer people a better "view of the world."

One does not need to look hard to run across other familiar wonders that exist because of some engineer's handiwork.

The very symbol of America, the Statue of Liberty, stands because of a structural engineer. Its structural framework was designed by Alexandre Gustave Eiffel, designer of the symbol of Paris, the Eiffel Tower.

SEVEN WONDERS OF MODERN WORLD

Because of the public's fascination with the spectacular, NEW offers an appropriate event to call America's attention to some of the spectacular engineering achievements — man-made monuments of such grandeur we view them with wonder and awe. They uplift the human spirit.

What are some of the monuments — super structures of the world — made possible by the skill, intelligence and daring of the engineer? Let's look at some of the most remarkable things ever built in this century, then go back in history to the beginning.

In tribute to the greatest engineering achievements of the 20th century, the American Society of Civil Engineers (ASCE) did a worldwide survey to chose the Seven Wonders of the Modern World. These international wonders — which demonstrate modern society's ability to achieve unachievable feats, scale what some thought were unreachable heights and scorn the notion that "it can't be done" — were selected from a long list of potential candidates. They all exist because of the creativity of engineers. The final list — the Seven Wonders of the Modern World — is shown in the table below.

Seven Wonders of the Modern World
1. The Chunnel (the tunnel between England and France)
2. The CN Tower (Toronto)
3. The Empire State Building (New York)

4. The Golden Gate Bridge (San Francisco)
5. The Itaipu Dam (Brazil/Paraguay)
6. The Netherlands North Sea Protection Works (Netherlands)
7. The Panama Canal (Panama)

Restricting the survey to man-made wonders located in our country — the Seven Wonders of the U.S. — the list includes: Hoover Dam, the Kennedy Space Center; the World Trade Center, the Trans-Alaska Pipeline; the Brooklyn Bridge; two previously mentioned as world wonders, the Golden Gate Bridge and the Empire State Building.

To hammer home that these engineering feats are regarded as wonders by even non-engineers, consider a piece written in 1995 by nationally syndicated columnist George Will. "Hoover Dam: Monument to What America Once Was," read the heading of the piece which called attention to the 60th anniversary of the Hoover Dam project. It read "Let us now praise those who conceived and executed this still-breathtaking marvel in the Black Canyon. The Dam is named for the president who was an engineer and who encouraged the project."

Hoover Dam was completed, Will added, "before it was considered correct to be a conscientious objector to the 'conquest' of nature; when America had an appetite for big conquering projects." He highlights a few other engineering exploits that, in his opinion, are of like significance including the Interstate Highway System, the Golden Gate Bridge and Apollo 13 which "fulfilled a government vow made in 1961."

In compiling its list of marvels, ASCE received nominations from engineering societies and distinguished engineering experts from around the globe. The final consensus list was judged on such factors as pioneering of design and construction, contributions to humanity and engineering challenges overcome.

The list of modern wonders evokes the storied Seven Wonders of the Ancient World, which first illustrated humanity's fascination with engineering works that seemingly defied the limits of nature. While only one of the original seven wonders remains, the modern wonders still stand for all to admire. They take their place in representing the engineering profession's legacy to the fast-closing 20th century.

For those who need to be reminded, the original Seven Wonders of the World (the ancient world) include the Pyramids of Egypt, Hanging Gardens of Babylon, Statue of Zeus at Olympia, Colossus of Rhodes, Temple of Artemis (Diana) at Ephesus, Mausoleum of Helicarnassus and Pharos Lighthouse at Alexandria. (See accompanying table — the wonders of the middle ages are also shown.) These masterpieces were extraordinary and admired for many reasons including their size and splendor. To protect the Zeus monument from the environment, it was housed in one of the world's first truly controlled buildings. Both the statue and its enclosure were designed by Phidias, who was not only highly regarded for his engineering talents but also considered the greatest artist of ancient Greece. He is credited with contributing the design of the Acropolis in Athens.

Seven Wonders of the World (Antiquity)
1. Hanging Gardens of Babylon
2. Pyramid of Khufu at Giza
3. Temple of Diana at Ephesus
4. Statue of Zeus at Olympia
5. The Colossus of Rhodes
6. Mausoleum of Helicarnassus
7. The Lighthouse at Alexandria

Seven Wonders of the World (Middle Ages)
1. Coliseum of Rome

2. Great Wall of China
3. Catacombs of Alexandria
4. Leaning Tower of Pisa
5. St. Sophia (Mosque), Istanbul
6. Porcelain Tower of Nanking
7. Stonehenge, Salisbury, England

The original wonders — all possible because of engineering — were, no doubt, amazing sights to behold. But today's modern wonders are even more awe-inspiring. They are not only artistically significant but truly functional operational masterpieces that have revolutionized engineering and benefited humanity. The modern wonders are a tribute to universal human desire to triumph over the impossible. (The seven modern wonders were featured in the December 1995 issue of *Popular Mechanics* magazine.)

DISTINGUISHED ACHIEVEMENT

Monumental engineering feats being planned and completed around the world are coming to fruition at an amazing rate. Many have the magnitude and significance of the wonders mentioned above, while some are more modest in scale. Still, they may alter our future and the way we do things. Many are engineering marvels in their own right.

One is the new Denver International Airport (DIA), a politically controversial $5 billion project when it opened in 1995. It exemplifies the difficulties in bringing to completion complex and highly visible public works projects in modern America. Even though it was touted early on as one of the "engineering marvels" of the decade — this nation's first new airport in 25 years — it was constantly barraged by the media and embroiled in one political fiasco after another. Because of its many leading-edge design concepts — for instance, it is the only airport in the world capable of simultaneous and parallel instrument landings by three aircraft at the same time — many thought it was too ambitious.

But after a rocky start, DIA now gets rave reviews, not necessarily from the national press but from those who count: the travelers (the actual users of the facility). It received the 1997 Distinguished Engineering Achievement Award, the highest honor of the American Society of Civil Engineers, the country's oldest engineering society. And, by the way, the "fiasco" DIA is also making the City of Denver a lot of money, way ahead of even the schedule that optimists forecast.*

DIA is only one of many projects the engineering community and this country can look to with pride. Consider the many new baseball parks built around the country, in such places as Denver, Baltimore, Cleveland, Dallas and Phoenix. Quite a few of these parks were built in the center of once deteriorating downtowns and have become the centerpieces of economic revivals there. They rank consistently ahead of older parks in attendance. And they wouldn't be standing if it were not for engineers.

Or consider the new extension of Interstate 70 through the Glenwood Canyon of Colorado, truly an engineering coup. The challenge was to take an old, winding two-lane road and make a modern freeway with a full four lanes through a spectacular mountain canyon — without upsetting the scenery or ecosystems in the process. The job was done so gracefully, protecting rather than disturbing the area's natural beauty, that people use the new route without ever noticing how difficult it must have been to build. Maybe that is the goal of any excellent engineering design.

What about things on the edge of tomorrow? Are we far from constructing a mile high building? Frank Lloyd Wright had one designed — at least preliminarily — in the 1950s.

What stopped him, among other things, was elevator technology; the structure could not be adequately serviced without taking up all the floor space just to house elevator shafts. Are we on the verge of solving this problem? I think it is conceivable.

How far in the future will it be before we have the bridge between Russia and Alaska that the world renowned engineer T. Y. Lin has promoted for years? Lin, professor emeritus of civil engineering at the University of California, Berkeley, has long said we have the technology but not the will to economically build and maintain such a structure. Lin, founder of an international engineering firm bearing his name, even has the plans developed to build what he calls the Peace Bridge. Maybe sooner rather than later, our children or grandchildren will be driving between the U.S. and Russia on vacation. Who knows?

The probabilities with the most potential adventure associated with them — as one looks into the new millennium and imagines what engineers will contribute — are those in space. After the success with Pathfinder — landing on, exploring and sending back never-before-seen images of Mars — we get goose bumps just thinking about what else we will someday experience in the universe. Certainly, anticipating what mysteries will be solved and discoveries made once we get data back from the Cassini spacecraft — one of the most ambitious probes NASA has ever launched — is as exciting as landing a man on the moon. Cassini, launched in late 1997, should reach Saturn in 2004. It will spend four years after that exploring the giant, ringed planet and most of its 18 icy moons.

CONSULTING ENGINEERING

What I've always found fascinating and loved about engineering is getting to see what I designed built and being used. There is a real sense of accomplishment — an exhilarating sense of pride — in seeing what you engineered come to life as a new product or system or, in my case as a consulting structural engineer, a new building or bridge or roadway. You, indeed, feel you have contributed and made lives better. You can point to a completed structure you are proud of and tell your children (and grandchildren) you engineered it. I guess that and the opportunity to be creative are the two most satisfying rewards of being in the consulting business.

Another is working in a branch of the engineering industry that closely reflects the changes in the world around us — seeing business trends, for instance, or the direction this country takes on environmental issues or trends in the construction industries. The ups and downs, shifts and slides in consulting engineering go hand in glove with public sentiment of the time. This gives one the sensation of being part of it all. Whatever the current demands-of-the-day are — cleaner air and waterways, more efficient highways and air travel, longer and wider bridges, taller, more intelligent and energy-efficient buildings — the demand for help to do something about the situation usually gets consulting engineers involved. If U.S. businesses are strong (and growing), that translates into a need for consulting engineers.

The consulting engineering profession in the United States began its ascension after World War II, growing in leaps and bounds to a multi-billion dollar a year industry. The trade association for consulting engineers, the American Consulting Engineers Council (ACEC), represents the majority of the consulting engineers in private practice, counting 5,500 member firms among its base. In 1995, these member firms had revenues of $14.6 billion and designed more than $100 billion in constructed facilities. (ACEC member firms employ approximately 200,000 engineers, scientists and technicians, nearly ten percent of the U.S. workforce of engineers.)

Let me indulge my own bias for a moment and describe some of the particulars of the consulting engineer's "world."

Independent businessmen and women

A consulting engineer is an independent businessperson who performs services for clients on a contract basis. Consulting engineers rarely have any commercial or manufacturing affiliations that might bias their judgment. They have nothing to sell except service, time and knowledge. Compensation consists solely of fees paid by their clients.

Consultants own and manage their own businesses. They operate as individual proprietors, in partnerships or as corporations. Their organizations vary in size from the sole practitioner and the principal with a few professional employees to firms with a thousand or more engineers, technicians, scientists, allied professionals and other employees.

Their services include investigations and analyses, pre-planning, design and design implementation, research and development, construction management and consultation on engineering problems. Consulting engineers are both advisors and problem-solvers, developing concepts as well as complete plans and specifications.

Professional licensing required

They are qualified to render their services by education, technical knowledge and experience. Consulting engineers are entrusted with protecting the public welfare, health and safety. Accordingly, the law requires they be registered professional engineers (P.E.s) licensed in the state (or states) where they practice, and where their design projects are located.

A consulting engineering firm serves a wide variety of clients. They include individuals; industrial, manufacturing and commercial concerns; municipal, state and federal governments; architects and other engineering firms; attorneys; contractors; developers; financial institutions; others with a need for engineering services.

Clients and fees

Fifty percent of ACEC member firms have a client base that consists almost entirely of owners and governments. With these clients, the firms act as prime contractors or "prime designers."

The remainder of the firms work mainly as "interpros" brought to a project through an "interprofessional" consulting contract. In these cases, consulting engineers work for other professionals, usually architects, "prime design" engineers or architectural/engineering (A/E) firms.

Consulting engineers work on an hourly or lump sum fee basis. Their fees may be determined on a percentage of the construction cost for the project they designed. Fees range from a few hundred dollars for a few hours of service to many thousands (even millions) of dollars for large projects. Consulting engineering services typically cost less than one percent of a project's total life-cycle cost.

Consulting engineers usually work independently in their own offices and, occasionally, in the client's office as an extension of the client's staff. Local, state and federal governments hire consulting engineering firms to work closely with their in-house engineering staffs. Because their work involves an almost infinite variety of projects, consulting engineers bring a wide range of experience and knowledge that in-house staffs may not possess.

Contracting-out, as described above, avoids having to maintain a large, permanent in-house engineering staff. This practice is also widely used by private companies set up primarily to perform general services, like industrial or product design. They occasionally require a particular expertise, such as mechanical, electrical or structural engineering. These companies or governments pay for the required, specialized engineering services on an as-needed basis. When the job is done, the private engineers are off the payroll until another need arises. Industry finds this to be quite cost effective; it helps to even out its peaks and valleys.

Widely diverse field

The private practice of engineering is a widely diverse field. Consultants are found in all engineering fields. Major fields include aerospace, agricultural, biomedical, electrical, chemical, civil, industrial, mechanical, mining and petroleum. Several subdivisions or specialties of the above disciplines also provide substantial employment opportunities for consulting engineers including automotive, environmental, geotechnical, structural and software-computer engineering. In a 1995 business survey of its members, ACEC found their primary fields of practice were civil (40%), structural (14%), mechanical (12%), environmental (10%), electrical (8%), geotechnical (5%), surveying (4%) and all others (7%).

Most of this country's infrastructure — highways, bridges, water and sewer systems, public building and facilities — not designed in-house by the engineering staffs of governmental bodies are designed by consulting engineers. The need for these services continues to grow, not only for designing new systems to meet the needs of a growing economy, but also to assess, maintain and even rebuild facilities already in place.

The design and construction of food processing centers, solar heating and cooling, coal gasification, saline water conversion, specialty manufacturing facilities, treatment plants and thousands of other similarly complex projects are normal everyday fare for consulting engineers. They may work alone or as part of a team. Frequently, these projects require more attention to zoning, machinery purchase and maintenance, markets, even financing and shipping issues, than to technical design and engineering. Engineering consultants contribute to such fields as health, sanitation, industrial production, transportation, public works, buildings, utilities and communications.

From the time the sun rises and people in industrialized society turn on the tap for a morning shower until they snap off the light before going to bed at night, they benefit in some way from the service of engineers in private practice. The generating stations that provide the electricity for cooking, lighting and a myriad of other electrical and mechanical appliances were probably designed by consulting engineers. The pure drinking water everyone uses but gives little thought to its source was likely supplied by water systems designed by consulting engineers. Likewise, consulting engineers are heavily involved in designing the majority of our office buildings, factories and schools.

Another major field for engineering consultants is in the operation of manufacturing or processing plants. Consulting engineers participate in projects that involve process engineering, production engineering methods, tooling, time and motion studies, and quality control.

Consulting engineers are also involved in the design of guidance systems for rockets, missiles, airplanes and automobiles. And they are involved in the design of conveyor systems, such as those used for airport baggage and at amusement parks, etc.

Often they are requested to testify as expert witnesses in court proceedings and advise clients and attorneys on engineering matters in legal disputes. A number specialize exclusively in court work, particularly in the fields of valuation and rate making, and forensic engineering — reconstructing failures, traffic accidents and even catastrophes like the TWA 800 crash in the summer of 1996.

Some consulting engineers only work in the patent arena. Others are engaged in work related to financing and feasibility studies for financial institutions. Some handle research problems and aspects of product development including the fabrication of devices, machines, instruments and equipment. Others test products and materials. Several are safety engineers, communications engineers or acoustic engineers. And the list could go on.

The thrill of challenge

Consulting is not for a person who hesitates to face new problems. The competent engineer who likes variety and enjoys the challenge of ever-changing problems can find a fascinating and satisfying career as a consulting engineer. Because major projects handled by consulting engineers include practically every kind of structure or facility that is planned, designed, constructed or operated, all branches of engineering are involved.

The consulting engineering profession demands business and management ability in addition to engineering and professional talent. It offers a unique opportunity for self-employment. It is perhaps the only path open to an engineer with the spirit of an entrepreneur who wishes to become his or her own boss in full-time engineering work.

Credibility

Rarely, however, do recent graduates start their own consulting engineering businesses. The two main obstacles are the requirements of the licensure laws and the establishment of credibility. To become a registered professional engineer, most state statutes require that a graduate of an ABET accredited engineering college work under the direction of a P.E. for a minimum of four years, then pass a written (plus, in certain states, an oral) test. To establish credibility, an engineer aspiring to be a consultant, must have years of experience and/or expertise in a specialty with a proven track record.

Business development

Perhaps the most difficult aspect of private practice is not gaining engineering expertise or getting licensed but gaining the ability to do effective marketing — the development of clients. To obtain commissions in the face of competition, consultants need to maintain a continuous sales effort through a cogent marketing plan that acquaints prospective clients with their talents. Some cling to the illusion that clients come to consulting engineers without any activity on the latter's part; one just needs to "hang out his or her shingle."

Sales activities consist principally of contacts with prospective clients, supplemented by brochures and other communication tools. Earning a good reputation based on competence and experience is critical. Every consulting engineer wants the maximum number of repeat engagements from the client he or she has served. Repeat engagements are a potent factor in building a reputation, for they signify that former work was completed to the satisfaction of the client.

However, while superior performance is the basis for repeat engagements, the consulting engineer also needs to maintain contact with former clients. Often there is a long period between a client's need for engineering services. During this lag time, consultants cannot rest entirely on previous performance. By keeping in touch with the client, they can learn of coming needs and remind the client, from time to time, of the quality of the previous work, current availability and interest in future work. (Marketing strategy is discussed in detail in Chapter Ten.)

The above description of the consulting engineering field touches on why many see engineers as wealth creators. By looking over the activities and range of services they provide, one sees a litany of the items that make America's quality of life (and the world's as well) what it is. That's why engineers are so vital to its continuation and improvement.

THINGS WELL DONE

I've never be able to read Emerson's words: "the reward of a thing well done, is to have done it" — without thinking of engineers — all ten or so million of them around the globe. What other group is there, with so many outstanding and extremely intelligent men and women, so intensely dedicated to activities adding value to humankind — and improving the conditions on this planet — uppermost in their minds? Money, fame and glory are secondary. Their reward for producing and contributing to the creation of wealth for all is using their minds — ideas and talents — to do it. We salute them — the engineers — for making things better. Someday, if enough engineering leadership comes forth to inspire it, maybe even the public will join our salute of our profession, and recognize engineers and our considerable accomplishments with all the fervor now showered on sports stars and screen celebrities.

9

WOMEN ENTREPRENEURS

"To succeed you must know what you are doing, like
what you are doing, and believe in what you are doing."

—Will Rogers

In 1986, only 4 percent or 1 in 25 American engineers was
female, according to the National Science Foundation. That
number is now 8.5 percent. Sheila Widnall, Secretary of the
U.S. Air Force (the first women ever to hold that position), stated in 1995, "Women today constitute 45 percent of the U.S.
work force, but only 16 percent of all engineers and scientists
employed in this country."

She finds those statistics to be woefully inadequate and
believes one answer is to interest young women in engineering
and science early in school. "We need to continue the emphasis
on precollege science and math education for all children, with
special emphasis on disadvantaged groups," she says, "At
decision points all along the education continuum, teachers,
counselors, advisors, and mentors can and should influence a
young person's math and science interests, and clarify career
options."

If more young women do, indeed, become comfortable with and start taking science and math courses early in their schooling, the number of women entering the engineering field could rise significantly. The movement may, in fact, be underway. Last year, women represented nearly 20 percent of all first-year, full-time B.S. candidates in engineering, according to the American Association of Engineering Societies.

MENTORS AND ROLE MODELS

As Widnall pointed out, mentoring has much to do with one's choice of a career. Equally as important is having role models in the field that interests you. Many unsung heroines in engineering have fought the odds and succeeded in what is still a male-dominated profession. Widnall herself, though she is hardly unknown or unsung, is one of those heroines and role models. She is an inspiration for women of all ages. Who are some others?

The following women are outstanding not only because they are successful in the field, but also because they are entrepreneurs — running highly successful respected companies — some of which were founded by them. Women-owned consulting engineering firms across this country are setting impressive track records in the male-run design/construction hierarchy. Their pace-setting efforts pave the way for more women to pursue engineering as a career. And this in the long run will do much to strengthen and elevate the profession as a whole.

WHO'S GEORGE?

Don't ask for "George" when you phone a certain consulting/civil engineering firm in Houston. The boss is *Georgia* A. Wilson, P.E., and she still gets calls from prospective clients asking for "George."

As a female engineer, the founder of Georgia A. Wilson & Associates, Houston's first female-owned consulting/civil engineering firm, is often reminded that she's a trailblazer in the predominantly male world of engineering. But she feels that's changing. A larger percentage of female scholars are on track to become engineers and lend their problem-solving skills to helping rebuild America's vital but crumbling infrastructure, and accomplishing other important engineering feats.

For some time now, women have been influencing the way America's consulting engineers do business. As more female professionals move into top management positions, they offer a different perspective on business and a more nurturing, interactive leadership style. And as more women begin to smash glass ceilings, the profession's male leaders are changing their attitudes. Many are learning valuable new lessons on how to be even more successful in business.

The company which Wilson, now a young 46-year-old grandmother, founded 15 years ago was cited as one of the nation's top 100 growing companies in 1995. Despite her busy work schedule, she finds time to volunteer several weekends a year to renovate homes for disadvantaged families. Several times she has traveled to Belize with her church group to help renovate schools.

To succeed, women consulting engineers such as Wilson say they must still go the extra mile as problem solvers and innovative business leaders. They must be as technically competent, competitive and creative in operating profitable practices, marketing their services, reaching out to their profession and the public, and advancing the technologies that improve the quality of American life. Many must balance their careers with motherhood, child-care and other family responsibilities that frequently go with being female.

WHY ENGINEERING?

As a schoolgirl in Texas, Wilson always liked to create, design and build projects. Her fascination with solving problems and "seeing a final product" — like an ambitious ninth-grade science project (i.e., an Orsat-gas analysis apparatus) — sparked her interest in engineering. Highly competitive, she enrolled as the sole female engineering student at Lamar University, Beaumont, TX, where she earned her civil engineering degree in 1973.

For Kristy Schloss, there was never any doubt she would become an engineer. Both her father and grandfather were engineers. They were her role models — as was her mother who, though not an engineer, was a businesswoman of note, a senior executive with a major bank. Schloss says, "My parents always encouraged me to be anything I wanted to be. And because I excelled in science — I loved science and math — I wanted to be an engineer, even though few female high school students of my day selected it as a career."

Schloss is president of a 100-year-old company that designs and manufactures environmental equipment — a company her grandfather, then her father, worked for and eventually purchased, renaming it Schloss Engineered Equipment, Inc. (Denver, CO). Kristy has been instrumental in expanding its international operations. Even though she frequently travels around the world on business, she finds time to be a force in the community, setting an example for other young women who just may want to become engineers, entrepreneurs and leaders.

The following list includes a few professional groups she is active in: the Society of Women Engineers (she served as president of the Rocky Mountain Section and is now a national committee chair), the Engineering Advisory Board at the University of Colorado's College of Engineering, the Colorado State Board for Community Colleges and Occupational Education, and the Colorado Women's Chamber of Commerce Foundation Board. Nationally, Schloss serves on the National Advisory Council of the Small Business Administration (SBA) and the U.S. Department of Commerce Export Council.

As a high-school valedictorian, Judy Nitsch, P.E., of Boston decided to become an engineer because "I like to figure things out." She was told she would make a good nurse or teacher, but she was determined to pursue her passion for math and science. Starting as a math major at Worcester Polytechnic Institute, Nitsch switched to civil engineering during her freshman year and received her degree in 1975.

Today, she is president and co-owner (with civil engineer Lisa Brothers) of the six-year-old firm Judith Nitsch Engineering, Inc. in Boston, MA. With 52 staff members, their woman-owned-business enterprise generates annual revenues in excess of $2.5 million.

When she entered the predominately male profession in the 1970s, Nitsch recalls, "It was lonely being one of only a few women engineers. However, there were many more pluses than problems. People remembered me and I made good contacts, many of whom have helped my firm grow. Yes, there were obstacles in my firm's early days. Not everybody, including banks, treated us like a real business."

BEAUTY AND BRAINS

Miss Colorado of 1991, Colleen Walker, is a lighting engineer with her own company. An architectural engineering major, her first job was as a project manager for the Boulder consulting engineering firm Energy Service Associates. She spent much of her beauty-queen reign talking to schoolchildren, especially girls, about the wonders of math and science. Even today, Walker is frequently on the road lecturing at schools and community groups. She continues to serve as a highly visible spokesperson and role model for young women interested in pursuing nontraditional careers.

Why did she become an engineer? An aspiring actress and vocalist who also excelled in math and science, Walker started out as a speech communications major on a Fulbright Scholarship. However, she soon realized there was greater demand for woman engineers than more TV news commentators. Encouraged to pursue a technical career, she has never regretted her decision to become an engineer.

"I think the role of women engineers is solidly being defined now," she says. "Those of us who are now in the profession must be role models and make ourselves heard when we tell how engineering is an exciting and viable career option for women."

NEW GROUND

"Women engineers are continuing to break new ground in engineering, a male-dominated field," says Debbie Carroll, 33, co-owner of Carroll, Chapin and Arevalo, a small geotechnical consulting engineering firm in San Diego, CA. "Sure, we've faced many difficulties," she adds, "but we've learned to overcome them by doing our best. If you do a good job, people don't care what your gender is."

Twelve years ago, armed with a journalism degree and a background in marketing, Diane Creel joined Earth Tech, Inc. in Long Beach, CA. Today she is president, CEO, and chairman of the board of the 2,000-employee consulting engineering firm with 44 offices worldwide.

How did a marketing expert end up heading a major firm whose fiscal 1996 revenues reached $200 million?

"I believe that every business decision is fundamentally a marketing decision," explains Creel. "You can only sell what people are willing to buy, at the price they are willing to pay and where they want it. Having a marketing background has been extremely beneficial in my success as CEO."

Early in her career, Creel said she looked in the mirror every day and told herself, "I have to prove I am competent today.

"Unfortunately, in today's male-dominated engineering profession, women must still work harder and go the extra distance to prove their competency," she observes. "However, I find that technical and operating opportunities for women are much better today than when I entered the job market 25 years ago. If you're a good professional who is committed and dedicated, you will find opportunities regardless of your gender."

As a businesswoman, Robin Smith Godfrey, president and CEO of Scharf-Godfrey, Inc. (SGI), Construction Cost Consultants, Bethesda, MD., admits she has faced the usual impediments to success. A single parent with two children, she joined the 75-year-old consulting firm 20 years ago, working her way to the top by asking the right questions and finding the right solutions. Godfrey made herself so key to both technical and business issues that, just one year after she was hired, her employers dissolved their partnership and formed a new corporation with her as a co-owner. She credits her success to determination and hard work.

Looking back, Godfrey, now 58, recalls the many times when conversations changed quickly when she and other females would join groups of males.

"Some men just don't want to include women," she

observes. "However, being a woman has had advantages. I have been the principal-in-charge on many projects where men have been pleased to have a new player's point of view."

Since 1975, Godfrey has built her small suburban office into an international corporation providing more than $4.2 billion in construction services annually. This woman-owned business enterprise (with 35 employees and a second office in New York City) is known worldwide as a successful and profitable cost-control and value-engineering firm.

In today's economy, cost containment is critical, Godfrey observes, "and architects and owners need to know if their projects are realistic." For major projects, reliable cost estimates are a necessity and, as a result, her business is booming.

"I love what I do, and I am still in awe of what we do as a company," Godfrey says. Her enthusiasm is visible to her employees, many of whom have worked with her for more than a decade.

AGAINST ALL ODDS

Deborah Naybor, with stout-hearted courage, overcame several roadblocks in her journey to becoming a leader in a man's world. Naybor is a professional land surveyor. Her father, who was an alcoholic, died when she was 13 years old, and "her family was thrust suddenly into a survival mode. We had to watch our pennies," she says. She worked her way through college by cleaning classrooms, graduating with a degree in forestry at a time when that industry was overcrowded with 1970s environmentalists. She couldn't find work in her field. Because she had taken a few surveying classes in school, she took a job at a surveying company to make ends meet.

She liked being outdoors (one reason she wanted to be a forest ranger) and she quickly got enamored with surveying —

even though it is almost exclusively a "man's club." She says her biggest problem, however, was not any open hostility, but that her abilities were always in question. Naybor, who is petite, said when she was out in the field, her hair tucked up in her hat, she was often called, "boy" or "son." Naybor had serious doubts if she wanted to stick it out. When things seemed the bleakest, she discovered a role model who gave her the courage to go on.

Her boss (a male), who had always gone out of his way to encourage her to stay in the field, gave her an article about a successful woman surveyor — a registered (licensed professional) land surveyor — saying, "See, you're not the only lady surveyor in the state of New York." Naybor said she studied the lady's career (which was inspiring) but just knowing another women had successfully navigated the obstacles she was experiencing made all the difference. And she began to earn the respect of her co-workers by, she says, "stepping in where others feared to tread." On one winter job, she was out pounding stakes into the ground when it was 40 degrees below zero. On another, she waded through a stream where the water was waist-high, her transit held over head just like the men in the crew. "The word spreads that you try harder," she comments.

Naybor has now been in the business for 20 years, eight years as the owner of her own land surveying-land planning firm in Alden, NY. Today, she herself is an inspirational role model of note for women of all ages. Two of her firm's favorite projects are the aerial mapping of the Buffalo, NY airport and work on 28-miles of NY State Highway 219.

Naybor was one of six recipients of the prestigious Avon's Women of Enterprise Awards for 1997, a national honor authenticated by the Small Business Administration and more than 200 women's organizations. It is the only national award program that recognizes women business owners who have overcome adversity. "There's a courage, a determination, a certain spirit that all these honorees have in common," says Avon's Kathleen Walas. "There's something inherent in these women. They want to make other people's lives better because of what they went through."

The only recipient of the Avon Award from a technical field, Naybor was asked why she didn't go into engineering or surveying right out of high school? She says there weren't any role models to identify with, none of her teachers pushed it and "the exciting aspects of either were never mentioned." Additionally, her perception at that time was that "engineering was a very difficult field for a women and engineers did not make a lot of money."

SAVVY BUSINESSWOMEN

"As small business entrepreneurs, we must wear many hats and keep a lot of balls in the air," says Georgia Wilson. "Success is a combination of many elements: technical competence, hiring and retaining the best and brightest staff, competitiveness in pricing and delivery of projects, planning and programming all elements of work. But, potentially, the most important element is continually attracting and retaining satisfied clients.

"How you run your business depends on your vision for the future," explains Wilson. "If an owner desires to remain small and is content where the firm is, he or she will invest profits in different areas than if growth is a major objective. It's essential to hire and retain the best and the brightest women and men. Try to recruit employees who are better than those whom you think you can afford. And then provide continuous training to all employees — even top officials and managers. While computers are necessary, capable employees are critical.

"People are a firm's most valuable assets, and managing those assets is critical," she emphasizes. "If you realize that no one is indispensable, you treat everyone more fairly.

"We try to look three to five years ahead in our hiring process," observes Wilson. "By forecasting our market and personnel demands, we can stay ahead of the curve in both hiring and training. Promotion from within is very important to build loyalty with staff. This can be a viable option only if employees are properly trained and developed to meet the firm's future needs."

She recently sold her operation to a large international engineering firm and though the name Georgia A. Wilson & Associates, Inc. is now a thing of the past, Georgia is not. She continues to make her mark as one of the state's leading consultants, only now as an executive with a firm having a much larger range of engineering projects.

PUBLIC RELATIONS

"Network, network, network! That's how we've grown into a successful firm," says Boston consulting engineer Judy Nitsch. Women and men who go into business for themselves need to make contacts to grow. "People need to know who you are," she adds, stressing the importance of marketing, communication and public/client outreach.

To gain recognition, firm leaders must get involved in community and professional activities. As president of the Boston Society of Civil Engineers in 1986, Nitsch not only made valuable contacts but "validated my credibility as a serious professional and firm owner." Her service has not gone unnoticed: she has garnered five young-engineers awards from national and local professional societies. Nitsch is currently vice president of the American Consulting Engineers Council of New England.

When it comes to a successful firm's administrative operations, "the bottom line is the bottom line," notes Nitsch. "Firm leaders must understand finance as well as marketing and personnel."

Deborah Naybor, who, upon receiving her prestigious 1997 Avon Award, was cited for her dedication to community work — Girl Scouts, Ronald McDonald House, an association for the blind and numerous nonprofit organizations. She offers suggestions about public relations saying, "I believe that, once you get up the ladder of success, you should turn around and help others up." That does not mean, however, you should avoid receiving credit for being a good Samaritan. If you give something to your community, it will give back to you. She suggests, "It's not just about winning new jobs; the reputation for good works rubs off on others. Doing community service has made a big difference in the attitudes of our employees. Everyone chips in. It's a team attitude and it's great for morale."

PLANNING AND SUCCESS

Planning and programming are also essential for all elements of a firm's work. "The most successful ventures are well-planned," stresses Wilson. "Even if an unplanned event brings potential success, it is difficult to take full advantage of that opportunity without prior planning."

A sense of urgency and focus, both in-house and with clients, can keep your firm ahead of the competitive edge. "One of the keys to success is doing things quickly," adds Robin Smith Godfrey. "Make as much as possible fit your own time frame. Always keep focused on what you're doing. And," she emphasizes, "there's no substitute for long hours and hard work."

Everyone interviewed believes an engineer must always maintain the highest ethical standards. "It is important to be honest in everything we do — from scheduling major construction management projects to answering phone calls," Godfrey explains. "For example, when I'm busy at the office, my assistant won't lie on the phone and say that I'm out. Also, we admit our mistakes; we follow up immediately to rectify any errors but we never cover them up."

They all also agreed that, to run a successful engineering business, client satisfaction is the most significant ingredient for success.

"It doesn't matter what a firm's size is as long as it serves its clients effectively," says Diane Creel. "How well we serve them determines how successful we become. The firms that form partnerships with their clients will succeed, especially in a difficult business climate."

MY DAUGHTER AN ENGINEER?

Challenges facing consulting engineers in the next decade will go far beyond the technical know-how needed to get the job done, according to Creel. "The primary challenge will be our ability to lead our firms through difficult times."

Change is the one constant in our profession, believes Creel. Her solid background in marketing and business-development comes through loud and clear when she adds, "Leadership today means being able to make change happen by motivating people to look to the future of our companies and our profession."

"The explosion in scientific and technical language in this century is creating societies dependent on science and engineering skills," report futurists Jennifer Jarratt and Joseph Coats of Washington, D.C. "Worldwide prospects for consulting engineers are excellent but they will face tougher competition."

Women in particular may have an advantage as consulting engineers in the future as the workload places greater demands on communications and "people" skills. Good-old-boy networks may become obsolete in tomorrow's more culturally diverse engineering work force.

While more women are entering the engineering profession in the 1990s, they are still under-represented. Observing that only 3 percent of members of the American Association of Cost Engineers are women, Godfrey believes this tiny percentage is not due to women's lack of exposure to engineering, but because many women let their gender limit their dreams.

Over the past 20 years, Godfrey has worked hard to overcome the myopic views and stigmas associated with women- and minority-owned businesses. She has spearheaded efforts to train women and minority professionals because "it's my responsibility to give something back." As a nationally recognized leader in the construction industry, Godfrey recently served on a *Construction Business Review* panel regarding affirmative action issues. "Too many wrongs have not been righted," she concludes. "We owe it to others who haven't made it. Something needs to be done."

As diversity and affirmative action programs encounter renewed attacks and setbacks, the engineering profession continues to widen the participation of women and minorities in the workplace, according to the American Association of Engineering Societies' quarterly bulletin *Engineers*.

Godfrey's determination and actions (as well as those of all the others mentioned in this chapter) are on target with that famous quip by Margaret Thatcher from Great Britain — the first women in European history to be elected prime minister: "You may have to fight a battle more than once to win it."

LOOKING FORWARD

Looking toward the future, the 21st century will bring a changing work force within a more diverse workplace. It will also bring a highly competitive global marketplace, a market-driven profession, advances in socio-engineering, adoption of sustainable development techniques and new approaches to business management. All these challenges require that we have the largest possible pool of talent from which to draw qualified engineering candidates. Women consulting engineers will need to be ready to stand alongside their male counterparts to accept these challenges and help build a brighter future.

What women engineers — not only in the consulting field but in all engineering fields — have accomplished in recent times, as well as throughout history, should be a source of pride for the entire industry. Anything we do, individually or through our professional organizations, to encourage as many of the brightest young women as possible to choose the sciences and engineering as careers, will only enhance our firms and our work. And, I suspect, women will bring their own perspectives to what the world needs and how to provide it. It can only be good for everyone.

10

---

10 COMMANDMENTS
OF MARKETING

"The pessimist sees difficulty in every opportunity.
The optimist sees opportunity in every difficulty."

—Winston Churchill

W hen I first opened my office many years ago, I hung out my shingle, sat back and, because I was a good engineer, waited for clients to beat a path to my door. I waited, and waited...and waited. Nothing happened.

That is, nothing happened until I went out and developed client relationships — which came about by learning people do business with people they know. Or, to put it another way, people hire people (or buy from companies) they know and trust; they purchase products and services they perceive give them their money's worth.

Marketing professional services is like leadership; it is as much an art form as it is a science. There's more to it than just a set of rules or systems. However, certain generally accepted steps go into the art — things that must be present to make it successful.

The key is finding ways to identify who is busy and can use our services (or buy our products). In the consulting business, it means determining ways to get to know prospective clients — on a first name basis if possible. Additionally, and basic to the art of successful marketing, is being sure we have a product or service people want.

RECENT TRENDS

Marketing attitudes have changed dramatically within the design community during the last two decades as a result of the wide fluctuations in industry markets, increased competition, more sophistication on the part of clients and an unraveling of the "old-boy" network. Even the most reluctant professionals are being forced to develop marketing programs.

Ted Levitt, Harvard Business School marketing professor and widely acclaimed marketing expert says in his book *The Marketing Imagination* that the purpose of business is to get and keep a customer. To do that, you have to do what makes people want to do business with you. Then direct all of your energies toward that end.

A successful, nationally recognized marketing expert on the west coast says there are really only three rules to successful marketing. They're like the three rules of real estate: location, location, location. What are the California rules? Get the job, get the job, get the job! Action items — take action, get out there and do something!

I don't know what it is about engineers — something to do with our genes — but the thought of making a "cold call" completely turns most of us off. Maybe it's that we love our work so much, we want to just stay in the backroom, make computations and do good engineering.

It is like being the most fantastic, well-trained and expert football or baseball team around, and not having any games to play because nobody scheduled them. Who does that for us?

If you are the head of the firm, the buck stops at the top; it is your responsibility. As consulting engineers, we are businessmen and women — actually we are that first and engineers second. And, as acclaimed marketing and business experts say, the purpose of business is to get and keep customers. So how do we go about getting business?

What follows are specific guidelines for marketing. I like to call them the Ten Commandments of Marketing for Design Professionals (See Table 10A). I didn't find them etched in stone on a mountain; rather, I developed them through trial-and-error during the more than 30 years my firm has been in business. (Though presented specifically for design service companies, the concepts are universal and apply to the producers of products and others, as well.)

TABLE 10A
The **TEN COMMANDMENTS** **of Marketing**
I - Know Thyself **II - Know Thy Market** **III - Have a Plan** **IV - Involve Everyone** **V - Run a Business** **VI - Be Selective** **VII - Keep Strong Ties** **VIII - Follow Through** **IX - Be Prepared** **X - Stay Visible**

1.) *KNOW THYSELF*

Know who you are and what you can do well. Don't just talk about your strengths; put down in writing what you do, what you're good at (and what your weaknesses are) — what you want to get better at and/or expand into.

Somehow writing things down — rather than just talking about them — allows you to better understand yourself. It has a greater impact when you see who you are in "black and white".

Be specific about your capabilities (your strengths and weaknesses). It's of little use to merely say "we are structural engineers" or "we do structural engineering." Specifically define what you engineer — what types of projects — and for what types of clients — public, private, a combination or what? And don't disillusion yourself. It's wonderful to have dreams and aspirations; just make sure they are realistic and not illusions of grandeur.

In the story of Mohammed Ali and the airplane the former champ is on a plane going someplace and the stewardess is having a difficult time getting him to put on his seat belt. She finally gets her supervisor and Ali tells the supervisor: "Superman don't need no seat belt." The head stewardess quickly retorts: "Superman don't need no airplane!"

So it's okay to have dreams, just make sure you're careful with them — and that you're wearing your seat belt. Knowing what you do best helps you focus your energies so you go after projects you can do well — ones that you really want to do.

My firm, for example, doesn't waste time chasing large sewage-treatment plants because we simply don't have the in-house expertise — nor the desire — to expand in that direction. On the other hand, we are good at designing large buildings, parking garages and bridges. And we concentrate on those.

Perhaps the most effective marketing weapon you can

have is confidence. And knowing you are the best at something — or can do it better than most — certainly is a confidence booster.

We don't use the shotgun method in our marketing approach. We use the carefully aimed rifle method — shooting at a smaller target, trying to hit a higher percentage of bull's-eyes.

It's like the Yogi Berra yarn where he's ordered a pizza in a restaurant and the waitress asks him if he wants it cut into four pieces or eight pieces. Yogi says, "Better cut it into four; I'm not that hungry."

I guess we use the "Yogi pizza method." We go after bigger pieces and fewer slices. Narrow your targets to those jobs and clients that best align with your strengths and fit your ongoing goals.

2.) *KNOW THY MARKET*

Invest time and money in finding out, not just what is in vogue now, but what the future holds. Do business development on those jobs that fit both your short-term needs and your long-term goals — five to ten years, or even longer. It is also recommended that you market only the kind of work for which you have (or can develop) expertise and skill — and you want to do. Most importantly, be sensitive to burgeoning markets and aware of outdated areas.

To make sure you do not end up chasing rainbows, position yourself to respond to those businesses or industries that are strong, growing and have the potential of being around for the long run. Nothing feels more discouraging than one day waking up and finding you are an expert at something people no longer want or need. The buggy whip industry comes to mind.

Be aware that how you position yourself to go after government work requires a different game plan than one for private-sector work — they require different approaches. Your approach is also different if you want to work exclusively for a particular client type like architects — or contractors — or developers — or bankers — or highway departments.

How about geographic markets?

Design firms increasingly look at the whole world as their market. The United States, most say, is becoming more and more a service economy. Part of its strength in the world marketplace is its leading-edge service industries. With a major piece of that industry being the design community, you may want to do business development, not only beyond your local area in the U.S., but overseas. (This topic is covered in more detail in the next chapter.)

However, when scouting far-flung markets, find a local partner. This partner should be familiar with local rules, customs and design codes, as well as having established contacts in the region. Also make sure when shopping for foreign markets you deal with a country which has convertible currency.

As I mentioned, our firm does a lot of parking structures which are basically the same throughout the world. So, more and more, we explore the international marketplace for these types of jobs.

We have done over 80 projects overseas. All but a handful have been financially rewarding, mainly because we have always found a local partner or associate familiar with the local situation — construction industry, governing agencies and the people. That alone — knowing the local people — helps insure you will get paid.

That is the biggest caution I have about doing foreign work: make sure proper arrangements are made beforehand to get paid — and with convertible currency. You don't want to be paid in vodka or beets. We almost did one time — when we did a dairy in Russia — and it wasn't a pretty sight (even though the guys in our office thought it would be great to have a lifetime supply of vodka on hand). The engineering design game is tough enough by itself without trading commodities for cash.

3.) HAVE A PLAN

While this may seem obvious, many firms have not developed a plan or put their budget or marketing procedures in writing. They have no written goals or strategy.

Your plan should emphasize the importance of three things: repeat clients, referrals and doing good work.

Have a designated marketing team — action people — a team of players who call on clients and prospective clients. And a principal or partner should head up this team — someone who understands business development — and why it's needed to stay in business.

At my office, we have our marketing group divided into two teams. The first group helps look after on-going clients and makes sure we stay in the driver's seat for their future work. The second group is a pro-active marketing team made up of extroverts. They make cold calls, presentations and sales — and they are highly respected because they bring in 80 percent of our new projects.

Have a key person in charge because marketing is costly — typical marketing budgets for design firms are 5 to 8 percent of gross billings, with one-third going to direct costs and two-thirds to people costs. A second reason is that, without the dedication and enthusiasm of a leader in the firm, most plans fizzle and fail.

If you don't currently have a formal marketing plan and want to initiate one, start by doing a couple of simple, straight forward surveys. First, an in-house survey to find out your current mix of clients — what types of projects are most profitable and what types of clients you work well with. Then conduct a client survey to find out how they feel about your firm and services, and how you stack up against your competitors.

You may — to your surprise — discover that, while you think everyone in the known world is aware of your expertise in a certain area, many are not. From these surveys, many ideas will surface — suggesting what direction to take to establish your marketing program — one that makes sense for you and your future.

These surveys will help answer questions like: Do we need a marketing coordinator or a marketing director — and should this person be full-time or part-time? Should we have an office newsletter? Who should get it?

Responses to such surveys provide sound input on the direction to take — and methods to use — in letting clients (and prospective clients) know all they need to know and why yours is the best firm to serve them.

Our single most effective communications tool has been our office newsletter. We publish it on a regular basis and mail it to about 2,500 people. It is so effective, we get a hundred or more unsolicited calls from each issue. It helps us keep current and former clients — as well as potential new ones — updated on our projects, people and new services. We send it to individuals, not to firms, which forces us to continuously update our computer mailing list — ensuring we stay aware of changes in our potential customer base.

4.) GET EVERYONE INVOLVED

An architect — a client of ours — once told me the story of one of his employees who belonged to a church that was planning a new building. Every Sunday this person went to church and listened to sermons about fund raising for a new building. Eventually, an architect was hired, one of his firm's competitors! By the time people in our client's firm heard about the project, it was too late.

It was a large, high-profile building and his firm would have loved to have been selected to design it. The architect's response to his supervisors was: "I've been here five years and have always worked on commercial projects. I didn't know we could even design churches." This person should have been, but wasn't, involved in his firm's marketing effort. He didn't even know about his own firm's capabilities.

It is important everyone in your company, from the receptionist to the people in the back room to upper management, participates in your marketing plan. Emphasize that, without new work coming in, you could run out of projects — which will mean downsizing.

Keep all your people informed and enthusiastic by letting them know that the marketplace — business world — develops an opinion about your company from contact with each member of the company. And make sure clients (customers), too, develop a favorable opinion about your company from contact with everyone.

How they handle themselves at the job site or project meetings, even how pleasant your receptionist is on the phone, can sometimes make the difference if you get the job or not. We once lost a major commission because of this — because the person answering the phone not only didn't recognize a client by name, but was rude in the process. She told him nobody had time to talk to him because we were too busy getting out a big project.

She is no longer with the firm.

A cruel, hard thing to realize about your employees is that, if they do not fit into your marketing concept and philosophy of providing service and will not change their attitude, simply help them find employment elsewhere.

At our office, we ask our people to say "we", "our team", "our firm instead of "me", "you" or "they". We are part of the same team working together.

According to Tom Peters, co-author of *A Passion For Excellence*, John McConnell, the chairman of one of the best-run steel companies, does not have elaborate corporate procedure books. Instead, his company's stated philosophy is: "Take care of your customers and take care of your people and the market will take care of you." This type of thinking has earned McConnell's company a spot on Peters' list of America's Best-Run Companies.

5.) RUN A BUSINESS

If you own, run or manage a for-profit business, you must make money to survive. It does no good to turn out award-winning projects (or products) if every job loses money. Many engineers (designers) choose this career for the satisfaction of their accomplishments. However, to stay in business, you need to show a profit.

Likewise, good businesspeople relate to their clients' needs — knowing they also must run their businesses successfully. They are aware of their clients' costs, and help them get the most value for their construction dollar. Let your customers know you are not just a design professional, but also a business professional.

Make sure your fees are adequate for the service you agree to provide. That should be first and foremost on your list of things to check out. I'm reminded of the story about a structural engineer who had a bad-paying client — an architect. This engineer, upset that the "no-good architect" wasn't paying his bill, finally had enough.

So he cornered the architect, ranted and raved and generally unleashed his displeasure about the situation. Then he presented this astonishing proposition — that he would forgive the architect his debt if he would agree to use the engineer on all the architect's future jobs!

What is that old adage? Something about throwing good money after bad?

Which leads us to our next rule.

6.) BE SELECTIVE

Take only those projects for which you are qualified and that can be financially and professionally rewarding. As many have painfully learned, growth for growth's sake alone can be damaging to a company's reputation and its financial stability.

Wise, sound growth, on the other hand, is good business — good for the bottom line. And it allows you to compete for more desirable projects and better paying clients. An added benefit is that stable growth creates a better work environment that attracts, keeps and motivates young, bright talent; employees know if their company provides new opportunities.

7.) KEEP STRONG TIES

If any of these rules should be etched in stone and labeled a commandment, it is to keep strong ties with your clients (and your references). I can't underscore enough the value of referrals in this or any other business, nor caution you enough to remember your competition is not out there sleeping. If you have an excellent client (customer), don't put it past your competitors to try to attract this company for their own. Sometimes your competitors might even undercut your fees or steal your key employees if they think it will get them a client.

By staying in close touch (and on top of problems) with your customers, you'll have a better chance of keeping your good clients happy. Most of all, you'll have a better chance of retaining them as clients, no matter what temptations come their way.

So don't spend all your marketing budget on new projects and clients. Show your repeat customers you appreciate them — take them to lunch once in a while — send them a letter of thanks every so often.

By maintaining those on-going client relationships, it's not just their work that will come your way — but new opportunities may also surface. We received a project — right out of the blue — because we stayed in close contact with a former client, who used to be one of four main partners in the largest achitectural firm in the Rocky Mountain Region. He is now semi-retired, but still running a small office, Jack Lawler Architects. A former schoolmate of Lawler's, from the east coast, was looking for a structural engineer with seismic experience and, because he knew Lawler's old firm used to have an office in California — where everyone knows they have earthquakes, he contacted him for names of structural engineers.

Lawler not only told his friend about us, he sold him on our firm — convincing him we were the best. We were selected before we even knew we were being considered for the project — two good-sized hotels in Japan.

Now, not all our work assignments come that easy, but it's nice to get one like that every once in awhile. It sure makes us want to take good care of our established relationships.

8.) FOLLOW THROUGH

Studies show that 80 percent of all first contacts are not followed up. The initial time and cost spent chasing down leads is lost, which is a terrible waste of both energy and money. The failure to follow up on leads, proposals and presentations — or to deal fully with client questions and problems — is a sure-fire formula for missing out on business.

Keep calling potential clients on a timely basis, without becoming a pest. Learning the right timing and frequency for making contacts comes with experience — it is an art. Be quick to smooth the "ruffled feathers" of clients and customers so small problems do not develop into ones that sever a relationship.

9.) BE PREPARED

As professionals, our brochures, newsletters and direct mail pieces are always expected to be first-class. But these are just tools. The bottom line for marketing is action — not merely pretty graphics, but action — taking the necessary steps to obtain the commission.

Perfected proposals — and good presentation skills — often make the difference on getting the commission. So make sure you are ready for that interview — long before you walk into the room to face the interviewers.

We always practice for interviews and do "dry run" presentations. Sometimes we even video tape them. It's surprising for a lot of people to see themselves on a TV screen rolling up their ties, chewing their pencils or rocking in their chairs. Videos help presenters learn to eliminate these distractions.

Some homework into what a prospective customer really wants — many times it is not in their "request for proposals" — always pays off. Do enough research to find out what their "hidden agenda" is. Communications specialist Gary D'Angelo says, "Usually, if people lose a job they thought they should have had, it is because of the 'hidden agenda', not because of the technical or people agenda." He adds that finding this out is not difficult: "Talk to the client before you make your presentation. You need good listening and probing skills — how to read what is not being said."

There's a lot of competition out there. Spend time finding out hidden agendas before you prepare your proposal. Make sure it's a "wow" proposal — one that someone reading it would say, "Wow!" And do not wait until you are short-listed to start working on your presentation skills. Take one of Yogi Berra's other observations as an alert: "It sure gets late early out there."

10.) STAY VISIBLE

Your company may do wonderful work or have the greatest product, and the most talented people in the country. But that alone won't get you customers if they don't know about you, your company or your work.

Make sure you and your company (and product) are visible in the communities and circles your clients and customers move in.

How about the media? How do you get featured in the press? This is a whole subject of its own (covered in some detail in Chapter Four). Let's review a few recommendations here, in a slightly different light.

For marketing purposes, get exposure in the publications your clients read, and get featured on the radio and TV programs they listen to. Find out which ones they are, then make it a point to know the editors, reporters and news directors at each one. Learn about their interests and what they consider news. Keep in mind that *editors* determine what is news, not us.

What is considered news by them is not usually news about engineering or what we do. You have a better chance of getting comprehensive media cover if you designed a project (or house) for Madonna or Michael Jackson or some sports star than if your project is an outstanding engineering achievement. Always make sure the stories you forward to the media have a "hook" — something that will catch the attention of their readers, listeners or viewers..

Without a good "hook," most news releases about engineering projects have little chance of getting much "play." And it is really not totally the media's fault. They are overwhelmed with material from people wanting to get news about themselves or their companies in print. A good friend of mine, the former business news editor of the *Rocky Mountain News* (Colorado's largest newspaper), says he received more than 500 press releases a day — 500 per day! Most are tossed in the waste basket after being scanned for less than half a minute. Anything that makes ours stand out from the others — such as having readily apparent reader interest angle or "hook" — is critical.

When you do get a feature story or a bylined article published, it is a *victory*. Make reprints and send them to all your clients and prospective clients — to friends and relatives, mom and dad. Get them out where others can see them. They come across as third-party endorsements which, for marketing purposes, are the best kind possible.

In addition to working with the media, our company stays visible by being active in the community. Several employees serve on civic organizations: little league baseball and soccer groups, planning boards, etc., rubbing shoulders with business and community leaders who often serve on selection committees or influence decisions on them.

We have even successfully sponsored public forums — events where we, for instance, discuss the impact new construction has on the community. We once did a seminar on how all the new high-rises being built altered wind patterns in downtown Denver and how wind forces at the sidewalk level affect pedestrians. This particular event attracted tremendous media attention — extensive television, radio and print media coverage — because our discussions dealt with people issues, not engineering issues. The public was impressed that engineers would relate to them how engineered projects touched their lives and shopping habits.

MILESTONES

The "ten commandments" are milestones to follow for a sound marketing effort. But the most important message for the engineer-businessperson to remember is this: people do business with people they know and respect, and they purchase the products and services they feel give them the best value for their investment and money. Make sure those you want to work for, and with, know you and your company — and know what it does.

We all want to do good work. But to do so, we must first *find* the work and get selected for it. Just like championship baseball and football teams who need games to play to show their stuff, we need projects to engineer to show our skill.

And the key for this for engineers and other professionals is a well-developed marketing strategy — one that has as many people as possible from your company lining up the games. With that in place, we can really show how great we are at engineering (or whatever you do or produce).

And remember, if you're the head person — or if you ever want to be — the buck stops there (at the top).

11

PATHS TO INTERNATIONAL VICTORY

*"The people who get on in this world are the people
who get up and look for the circumstances they want,
and if they can't find them, make them."*

—George Bernard Shaw

As we speed headlong toward the new millennium, bombarded on every side by a radically new political reality worldwide, exploding technology, and unprecedented global competition, I see international work opportunities for engineers at every turn. Indeed, I see opportunities especially for the small- to medium-sized engineering firm located anywhere in the world.

To me, this recognition of vast global opportunity seems obvious. But in my travels throughout the world on engineering missions, I have detected a slight, yet troublesome, sense of apprehension on the part of my fellow engineers who look at the challenges ahead as overwhelming. This, I believe, is merely a case of not seeing the forest for the trees. Believe me, the forest is full of profit if only you take the right paths. And these paths lead *to* anywhere from anywhere in the world.

SIZE DOESN'T MATTER

For many decades after World War II, taking advantage of international work often meant getting big. The investment necessary to market to large governments and acquire technology to meet the demands of international work were enormous. Small- and medium-sized firms were at a distinct disadvantage to their multinational counterparts because of high costs associated with maintaining far-flung operations.

Today, however, the emerging technologies of the Internet make it possible for even the smallest concern to work on the world stage with relative ease. Design work done in, say, Chicago can easily be married to working drawings done locally — in India or Korea or wherever. Under this scenario, technology means that anyone can be global.

Another major change is exploding on the world stage. Governments throughout the world are decentralizing, a` la the former Soviet Union and the satellite nations of Eastern Europe. At the same time, governments all around the world, including the United States government, are privatizing operations. Also, governments and big business alike are less apt to maintain armies of in-house professionals, so the opportunities to bring in engineers of every stripe as consultants are more plentiful than ever before.

Taking advantage of these changes does not require vast resources, but it does require identifying the paths to take to international success. For the small- to mid-sized firms, this begins with taking advantage of the major strengths such firms bring to the table. Smaller firms most often have their principals involved in a "hands-on" manner, giving them the ability to make decisions quickly and react to opportunity when it arises. Also, since smaller firms are less burdened with bureaucracy, often they can meet tighter schedules, perform work faster and at a lower cost. In today's world, you can't overlook the edge that such flexibility offers to clients.

I have collected several case studies that illustrate how relatively small firms, both U.S.-based and non-American firms, have used flexibility, ingenuity and enterprise to garner work beyond the confines of their own country's boundaries or with firms from other lands.

MAKING CONTACT

To obtain international work, small- to medium-sized firms have to target their limited resources. Broad-based advertising or opening offices in foreign countries to seek out work is often prohibitively expensive and may not pay off in the end. We have to work smart and take full advantage of all strengths.

I have a friend, Brian Lewis, a professional engineer and a management consultant to engineers, who was planning a pleasure trip to New Zealand (NZ). In preparation, he sent out a few letters to design firms there, mixing a little business with leisure. He had been giving workshops on marketing engineering and architectural services in Great Britain — fifteen in the prior three years — and wondered if New Zealand architects and engineers might be interested in similar workshops.

In addition to writing private firms, he contacted the NZ Institute of Architects. It turns out his timing was propitious. They had just changed their by-laws to permit pro-active marketing by design professionals and they responded, requesting him to do workshops at three venues. Further serendipity arose when, at one session, a representative of the NZ Ministry of Works told Lewis the government had just decided to initiate privatization of the ministry's engineering and architectural design staff. He asked if Lewis would talk to them.

Through first initial informal initiative, Lewis was able to garner several advisory assignments over a ten-year period dealing with the government's privatization efforts. His work, he says, eventually "culminated in the sale of both a 1,200-person design consultancy and a $250 million (NZ) per year road construction company." This is the kind of enterprise (and commitment to a long-term effort) that building an international business base requires. It's one of many paths to international victory and success.

AN INDISPENSABLE EXPERTISE

Following the reunification of Germany, the new government set up a company called WISMUT GmbH to complete the decommissioning and remediation of uranium mines, mills and associated facilities in the former East Germany. WISMUT, seeking worldwide expertise in such matters, contacted a Canadian research organization, CANMET, for assistance. CANMET, in turn, referred WISMUT to a number of Canadian consulting companies that had experience in the areas of acid rock drainage and environmental issues in operating (and closed) mines.

One of those firms was Steffen Robertson and Kirsten (North America), Inc., a geotechnical/environmental engineering company with its head office in Vancouver, B.C. and branch offices in Denver, Reno and Columbia, SC. About half of SRK's staff dedicates its interests to consulting for mining industry clients.

Because it had an indispensable expertise in the needed specialty, SRK was asked to participate in workshops in Germany and discuss remediation measures that have been applied at uranium mines in the west. After the workshops, SRK was requested to submit proposals on a number of small projects being launched by WISMUT. By working with the client's engineers as much as possible and training them when necessary, the scope of SRK's work broadened.

In its first 18 months on WISMUT-related work, SRK

anticipates total billings that will approach $750,000 (U.S.). The firm is currently contemplating opening an office overseas to serve the central and eastern European markets.

STRONG CONNECTION TO AN OWNER

Another example of a small- to medium-size firm expanding to meet international markets involves my own company, Richard Weingardt Consultants, Inc. (RWC) of Denver, CO. This case came about because of a strong existing relationship with a principal in an international project.

A large New York-based international trading company contracted with three regional governments in Russia to build several cattle feed processing complexes. I had gone to school with the president of that trading firm and he called me for engineering advice. As a result, our firm was given the opportunity to present our credentials for the work. My staff not only convinced my old friend and his executives that RWC was up to the civil and structural engineering, but we were also selected to be the design team leader and program manager for all aspects of the projects.

RWC selected and directed all sub-consultants for the other necessary disciplines: mechanical, electrical, geotechnical, processing and related engineering. Our firm, under program management, also assisted with the purchasing, shipping and installation of U.S., European and Taiwanese manufactured products. The construction costs for the first three complexes were $29 million (U.S.) each. More than 50 similar projects have now been completed using our original design concepts.

LOCAL EXPERTISE COUNTS

Sometimes local expertise is the deciding factor. CO-ARCHI-TECTURE, an architectural and consulting engineering firm of Dar-es-Salaam, United Republic of Tanzania, responded to an advertisement in the African Development Bank publication about a 980 KM roadway project, Manyoni to Kigoma.

The firm researched the potential list of large, international engineering firms going after the project, and elected to contact Gannett Fleming, Inc. of Harrisburg, PA. CO-ARCHI-TECTURE presented its credentials to Gannett Fleming, was selected to become part of the team, and was involved throughout the project, from the feasibility study to the design and construction phases.

Moreover, CO-ARCHITECTURE assisted the Gannett Fleming team during presentations to obtain the contract, so they not only brought local African expertise to the project, but invested in marketing the work as well.

PERSONAL RELATIONSHIPS ARE EVERYTHING

Another example of globalizing comes from building personal relationships stemming from successful business partnerships. About 20 years ago, Turner International Construction brought in Lehr Associates of New York City to do a mechanical engineering peer review on a problem project: a large hospital in Pakistan. The original designers had made mistakes but, rather than "point fingers," Lehr suggested ways to salvage not only as much original design as possible, but also the local relationships.

The lead designers from the U.S. and Europe had Pakistani associates so Lehr inherited the local, domestic firm when it received the commission to do the modifications. The original engineer who was highly critical of the domestic firm's past performance — a view not shared by Lehr — was eventually dismissed. The owner and Turner International were so pleased with Lehr's work that, before the necessary engineering revisions were completed, the project was expanded. What started out as a peer review assignment ended up netting Lehr $2 million (U.S.) in final fees.

That business led to a strong personal relationship between Lehr and the Pakistani firm, a relationship that has resulted in numerous joint mechanical-and-electrical engineering projects in the region. Sometimes Lehr is the lead firm and sometimes the opposite is true. This successful example led Lehr to develop rewarding work and similar personal relationships with firms in Egypt, Japan and other countries.

DOMESTIC CLIENTS DEVELOP
GLOBAL PROJECTS

Another way to expand globally is to maintain close contact with domestic clients; you never know when an international opportunity for one of your clients will also open a door for you.

This happened to Houston-based Walter P. Moore and Associates, Inc. A senior executive of one of Moore's domestic clients took a new job with a company starting to develop projects outside the U.S. At the request of this executive, the Moore company was interviewed by the new firm concerning a project in Spain.

Moore was ultimately selected to be the structural engineer on the project and, along with other U.S. mechanical, electrical and architectural consultants, was asked to associate with a domestic Spanish firm. The firm and its Spanish associate are now involved in all phases of a project that will cost $200 million (U.S.) upon completion.

Using this experience, Moore has discovered that quite a number of its domestic clients are developing projects on the international stage. With Moore's expertise in associating with local partners in foreign lands, many U.S. clients are taking Moore along as the structural engineering firm wherever the project is located.

Additionally, some large U.S. architectural firms that Moore works with have used Moore for projects generated by their international offices. Once again, Moore's experience cooperating with a local, domestic engineering firm knowledgeable of local practices, customs and politics is paying off.

BEING IN THE RIGHT PLACE AT THE RIGHT TIME

When you think of international marketing, never discount the power of being in the right place at the right time. Of course, happenstance can be enhanced by enterprise.

In 1992, an executive of Loebl Schlossman and Hackl (Architects) of Chicago went to China and attended an executive committee meeting with members of the Architects Society of China. After the business sessions concluded, he met socially with several prominent local architects and the Director of the Architectural College at Shenzhen University and its Design Institute.

The following day, the director called the Loebl executive, saying he was impressed with the firm's brochure and the projects it had completed. He asked if Loebl would be interested in participating, along with the Design Institute, in a design competition for a new project.

At first, Loebl was reluctant, but decided to take part

after learning the client would pay a stipend for the firm's participation in the competition. The competition for the 2.4-million-square-foot project was limited to nine firms, three from China and the rest from around the world.

A jury of 30 people selected the Loebl entry as the first-place winner and, within months, Loebl was commissioned to design the facility. The project included a 68-story office tower, two 30-story apartment structures and an eight-story retail base. Completed successfully, Loebl has since designed four additional projects in China and plans on doing many more well into the future.

GOVERNMENT SUPPORT

Entrepreneurial engineers, looking at the global marketplace, may also want to check out the support certain governmental agencies, either federal or state trade development offices, have to offer. Fred Berger, vice-president of Louis Berger International, Inc., a large U.S. engineering firm (well-established in the international marketplace) recommends that American consultants planning to start doing foreign work become familiar with the U.S. Trade and Development Agency (TDA). He states, "The U.S. government used to be more aggressive in recognizing its responsibility in helping American firms compete internationally."

USAID, which used to have a large bilateral aid program and a strong infrastructure development focus, according to Berger, has reduced its assistance to the infrastructure industry. "The void has now been filled by TDA, a much smaller but very supportive export support-oriented agency," Berger says.

Many of TDA's studies delving into opportunities for the sale of American goods and services overseas begin with what it calls "definitional missions" which Berger says "are designed to cost less than $10,000 as a field study, and are reserved for small firms." Once a firm has gotten "in the door" on a smaller "definitional-type" contract, other work could flow its way. He says small firms should keep in mind that "'big engineering firms' weren't always big and weren't always working overseas."

Schloss Engineered Equipment, Inc. of Denver, CO has been successfully doing international business for more than 30 years. The company, which designs and manufactures environmental treatment equipment, is heavily involved in doing international trade with the Far East and the Middle East. Kristy Schloss, its current president, says her company's export sales have increased 900 percent during the past five years.

She credits the Colorado trade office for helping the company close deals, understand protocol and overcome cultural differences. She says, "Foreign trade is almost a necessity in our line, but negotiating with foreign executives can be frustrating at times. In the Far East, everything is a process of negotiation. It's not over until it's over, and even then, it's probably still not over!"

THE ART OF THE DEAL

The Crosby Group, Inc., a medium-sized, Denver, CO, architectural and systems design firm, has, like Schloss, a long track record of doing business globally. Some of its more lucrative work has been on projects they have instigated — deals they have put together. When quizzed about how many of the aforementioned "paths" he used in his operations, Roger Crosby, TCG's president, answered, "All of them!" The following, in his words, is what he calls the "art of the deal."

"Moving into the global consulting market for our small company was a natural extension of the work (and philosophy) we were already doing for our domestic clients. In the early 1970s, the mainframe computer industry was accelerating and corporate management began to realize that the protection of this high value equipment, the data and its sensitivity to environmental problems required a special type of facility. Recognizing this new market, I focused our marketing efforts on providing data processing and telecommunications facilities.

"In late 1978 and 1979, the space industry began developing the first private satellite network. We were lucky enough to start working in this area, primarily because it was a natural step from data centers.

"I have always felt that the best way to assure my company's success was to demonstrate to our prospective clients that we had a special skill set that they needed to accomplish their projects. In order to separate ourselves from our competition, I decided to write a book and start giving seminars on the subject of how to design and plan data processing and telecommunications facilities. It worked very well. Speaking for an international facilities management association, I presented six seminars in six states over a period of two years. This exposed me to nearly 240 companies. Any marketing effort which allows you to get in front of that many possible clients that quickly is fantastic.

"The seeds we sowed during the early years set the stage for creating 'an indispensable expertise' in the areas of computers, satellites and telecommunications. Every consultant I know tries to establish a 'strong connection to an owner' doing nearly everything they want, large or small, when they need it and, most importantly, *whenever* they need it. I found that, by being willing to go wherever the client needed us, we succeeded in getting the strong connection to the owner we wanted.

"'Personal relationships are everything'. How true, how true. By having constant and close communication with the owner, you are privy to confidential information before anyone else, being at the right place at the right time. This is where it can get very interesting and has allowed me to create work for my company. That's right, create work! By being a good listener to my client, I frequently hear what new programs, products and/or services they are planning to keep their company vital, successful and growing.

"By listening carefully to the client, I try to understand where he is headed and, over the next few days (sometimes weeks), I find new ways we can fit into their planning. Oftentimes a piece of architecture is not what they need; instead, it's project management assistance. Creating solutions to their problems is what I do best. My clients are no different than anyone else; they are overworked and need someone to make their life easier and assure their continued employment.

"We market primarily to U.S.-based high technology companies who are aggressively selling their products or services internationally, and need consultants willing to go wherever they are needed. Paramount to our success is correctly assessing problems and keeping the client informed about the cost, time and effort required to realize their goals. But above all else, we are always watching out for the client's best interests.

"As an example, here is how I created a business opportunity for my firm using *all* the ingredients (paths) Weingardt mentions. Four years ago a large, high-technology telecommunications company announced plans to build the world's first 100 percent digital multi-channel television facility which would compete with cable television using satellites. This $600 million (U.S.) effort involved building and launching two high powered satellites, each valued at approximately $180 million and building and equipping a new state-of-the-art Broadcast Operations Center (BOC), expected to cost approximately $120 million. The project has been widely successful, and we were the architects and engineers of the BOC.

"As the years have gone by, several companies have built similar systems and we were selected to design those facilities also. To date, we have completed four and are working on the fifth, two in the U.S., one for Latin and South America, and one in Malaysia. The newest one will be built in Thailand.

"However, this is really just the beginning of our 'new opportunity.' It occurred to me that small multi-channel television facilities could be built using state-of-the-art technology anywhere in the world if a few key things happened. First, someone needed to launch a high-powered satellite that would cover huge geographic areas and would be willing to lease single transponders to these small countries. Secondly, a complete 'turnkey' solution could be offered, combining the skills of several international companies having experience in this field. Then perhaps a global multi-channel television system could be made available to even small countries and/or companies.

"Organizing this has proven to be one of the most interesting experiences of my life. I first drafted a concept paper and began discussing the idea with an international satellite provider who has 139 countries as member/investors.

"They decided that building two high-powered satellites was feasible if, and only if, they could pre-lease the preponderance of the capacity prior to launch. This they have done.

"Next, I convinced one of the world's largest electronics companies that there was a global opportunity to sell its set-top boxes and small aperture dishes if it participated with our team. Thankfully the decision makers agreed. In addition, we needed an RF uplink and downlink antenna manufacturer and, most importantly, a company experienced with setting up and managing Customer Call Centers and the ever complicated Subscriber Management Systems. Our firm will provide the architectural and engineering expertise to plan, design and help build (with local A/E assistance) the new broadcast facilities required to support this new service.

"At the time of this writing, six countries are in active negotiations with us to have 'turnkey projects' provided. This is really exciting. I am convinced this concept will allow us to assure my company's continued work load for many years to come. And, after all, this is what it's all about — having the creativity to apply your special knowledge to a client with a need, who wants to work with someone they have a personal relationship with, is willing to go anywhere in the world, enjoys working with local people in foreign countries, is flexible enough to understand the long view and is willing to do whatever it takes to help make the client successful in its enterprise."

DEMONSTRATED SUCCESS

I call attention to these examples (and paths to victory) specifically to show how international success wasn't dependent on large expenditures for marketing and/or having a foreign office.

They demonstrate how good fortune presents itself when we take advantage of opportunities: an indispensable specialty, strong ties with the owner/financier, local expertise, personal relationships, domestic client opportunities, and making contacts worldwide at meetings and conventions. Virtually every firm, no matter what size, can tap these strategies.

If one doesn't look promising, then explore another, always keeping in mind that opportunity most often knocks on the door of the firm enterprising enough to seek it out. And always remember to empasize your major strengths as you focus your efforts.

Also, keep an eye out for international opportunities arising out of the changing world. As my colleague Roger Crosby so ably noted, engineers and architects don't have to limit themselves to design work. Sometimes considerable success awaits us in putting the deal itself together.

I see new and/or expanded needs for engineering work worldwide in many fields and areas including environmental management; security system design for terrorism; software engineering; guidance systems for highways, airports, and mass-transit; bio-engineering (artificial body parts, pacemaker-types of products, advanced laser surgery); pollution control devices; more efficient operation of facilities; inventorying infrastructure (age, condition, replacement dates, etc.); maintenance and repair of highways; program management.

With all the technological, geo-political and business changes exploding every day and portending to continue at an even greater pace, many paths to international success for the enterprising engineer can be taken. To again borrow from Yogi Berra: "When you see a fork in the road, take it!"

12

PARTNERING WITH GORILLAS

"Wise men don't need advice. Fools won't take it."
—Benjamin Franklin

Dramatic changes are revolutionizing progress in America — how we get things done, manufactured and constructed. How these changes are affecting the building process typifies the situation. What it takes to get something completed in today's built-environment, for instance, is much different now than it has been in the past. It is not just that construction projects and ventures have gotten so much larger, more complex and sophisticated. Plenty of skill, talent and expertise exists (or is evolving) to deal with those issues. No, what is slowing down, adding unnecessary costs and often killing construction projects mostly comes from outside the design and building industries — and not all of it is bad — though I frequently have difficulty finding the good in (or benefit of) many of the "slower-downers."

Obviously the litigious nature of our society is one culprit. But there are other roadblocks caused by a proliferation of regulations, zoning and control codes, and no-growth legislation as well as the number of agencies, governmental bodies, citizens' groups and other controlling entities whose approvals must be obtained. The difficult nature of financing major undertakings, especially the ever-increasing (and much needed) public-private infrastructure projects, is another factor.

THOSE LIKE US

Attacking these problems and having some control of our own destiny will require that engineers get involved in shaping the public agenda, its values, policies, laws and regulations. We cannot do it alone. We must partner and team with others, and the easiest teammates to find are those in our industry or related industries. And one place to start is by partnering on activities to deal with the forces affecting our businesses — and improve the conditions within our own sphere, as Teddy Roosevelt encouraged. Hopefully that will lead to working together with broader groups and on broader issues.

As an example of partnering — tenets of which could apply to any industry or activity — let's look at efforts now underway in the design and construction industry regarding the built-environment. We will concentrate on the ongoing and yet always-changing relationships between architects and engineers (A/Es).

ENGINEERS AND ARCHITECTS

Traditionally, architects are the lead designers on all "people" buildings, e.g., health care, educational, office, residential and public-assembly facilities. Considering themselves "master builders" responsible for the whole building process, architects relied on consulting engineers to make their aesthetic "masterworks" functional. Consulting engineers often took a back seat, hidden from public view, except when designing power plants, water treatment facilities, industrial facilities, infrastructure, and other civil projects. That is beginning to change.

In today's sophisticated "people" buildings, an "aesthetic statement" is often not the top priority. Buildings must be engineered to be energy efficient and cost effective as much as they need to look good, fit their sites and blend harmoniously with their surroundings. With increased demand for multiple-use, environmentally sensitive, people-accessible, and/or "intelligent" buildings, more engineers are assuming the lead design role as catalysts in the problem-solving process. This is especially true when refined engineering systems comprise a major part of the work, e.g., manufacturing and processing plants, intricately technical laboratories, warehouses and parking garages — or when an engineer's expertise for project management is stronger than the architect's.

This is not a design competition between architects and engineers, but a nurturing of broader partnerships between major players of the building design equation: partnering or "teaming" as a means to meet complex, modern-day design needs.

COOPERATION AND COLLABORATION

In view of many roadblocks hindering the initiation and completion of successful building ventures, the changing roles and responsibilities within the construction industry, and the emerging importance of stronger design teams, a new era of cooperation and collaboration is taking shape across the country, and world-wide.

In 1993, the American Consulting Engineers Council (ACEC)) and the American Institute of Architects (AIA) signed a partnering agreement to work together to advance each other's common causes. The agreement,"A Call for Action: AIA/ACEC Joint Statement of Mutual Goals" was prepared to resolve differences that divided the two professions and, subsequently, diminished their traditional ability to lead the construction process. To improve the business environment, professional capabilities and economic vitality of A/Es, the two organizations agreed to:

- Improve communications between the organizations, their members, and the public.
- Enhance the leadership of engineers and architects within the construction process.
- Support increased use of qualifications-based selection (QBS) procedures for procurement of professional services.
- Improve project quality and profitability.
- Establish a process for problem-solving at the national, state and local levels.
- Encourage joint ventures in continuing education related to business practices.
- Enhance respect between architects and engineers, and encourage an understanding of each discipline's professional practice.

Subsequently in 1994, ACEC, AIA, and the National Society of Professional Engineers (NSPE) issued a statement of inter-professional cooperation recognizing "our common interests in protecting the public health and safety by providing professional design services to the public. We represent different professions responsible for the built-environment and specifically seek ways to work together to reduce conflicts within the broader community. We oppose inter-professional jurisdictional disputes between architects and engineers (on issues like who should be the lead designer) as being counter-productive to the interests of the public and the design professions."

In this regard, ACEC supports an open-market concept whereby the client selects the best qualified prime designer, whether it is an architect or engineer. It is the client's choice. ACEC states, "We cannot afford to use professional licensing laws as a device to carve up potential markets." Engineers and architects are both licensed as professionals to protect the public welfare, health and safety. We are expected to deliver the highest quality design possible whoever the lead designer is. To accomplish this we must heighten the level of teamwork within the A/E community; partnering is needed.

"Design and construction is not an adversarial process. It is one of team-building," according to James Lawler, a former president of AIA. Partnering is part of that but, he stresses, "Partnering is more than a series of formal meetings between teammates; it is an attitude based on trust, open communication and shared vision."

BUILT-ENVIRONMENT PARTNERING

Among federal government agencies, the biggest proponent for partnering on built-environment projects is the U.S. Army Corps of Engineers. When asked why, General (Ret.) Henry Hatch, former head of the Corps, responded, "The essence of partnering is to promote a cooperative attitude and the active pursuit of common goals by all parties involved." That is the best way to insure the best projects for the money.

ACEC and AIA look at partnering as "a way of doing business that helps the providers and recipients of services work together to achieve both their mutual goals and objectives." Partnering fosters cooperative attitudes within both professions, allowing them to provide better value to their clients and meet today's demanding challenges in the current business climate and global marketplace. True collaboration between A/Es is ever-increasingly needed, if they are to be a match for the ever-increasing economic, societal, technological and legal demands facing them. It is the only positive thing to do to get design and construction projects completed on time, within budget, and to the client's satisfaction.

BUILDING FENCES OR MESHING TALENTS?

The two professions have always been partners in the building process, but they have not always worked together in harmony. There have been the turf battles and instances when the prime designer (whether architect or engineer) has treated its team members poorly. This must stop. The dramatic changes revolutionizing the building process today will destroy us both if we don't. To remain strong (and become stronger) players in the design of the built-environment, we need each other more than we admit.

If consulting engineers and architects don't work cooperatively, we run the risk of being hired by someone else as subcontractors and losing control of project design altogether. On the other hand, by banding together we bring the ultimate design and management expertise to the table, assuring owners that all aspects of the project — engineering, architecture and the proper execution of each in construction — receive equal and top-level attention.

AIA's 1995 president, Chet Widom, commented that A/Es are "not an accidental collection of warring cells — that's what a cancer looks like." He added, "We must become, by necessity, a mutually supportive, collaborative industry. In this complex society, no single one of us has the knowledge to do it all. Will there be disagreements? Of course. But they are, in reality, only a small element of our relationship. We must agree to disagree on that 5 or 10 percent, then get on with the 90 or 95 percent of the issues that relate to our common good."

"We can learn from each other," states consulting engineer George Dunham, past chair of ACEC's Inter-Professional Committee and head of a multi-discipline engineering company in Rapid City, SD. To strengthen ties between the design professions at all levels, he suggests we should encourage "liaisons between AIA and ACEC at the local and state levels as well as nationally." Problems continue because people doing the work don't sit down and negotiate resolutions."

San Diego engineer-architect Joseph Paoluccio, CEO of PWNA, underscores the need for both sides to communicate "more often and better (orally and in writing)." Consulting engineers and architects must be involved in the planning process together, he says. "Not from the standpoint of the architect doing a design and the engineer making it work," he adds. "It has to be a symbiotic relationship. Mechanical engineers (as an example) should meet with the owners to understand their needs. Architects leading the project must tell their client, 'If you have humidity-control problems, I'd like you to meet my engineers.'"

"Wonder-teams" of architects and consulting engineers enjoyed a more symbiotic relationship back in the 1950s and 1960s, Paoluccio recalls. The building process became more complex as more developers entered the picture, paving the way for larger contracting firms to take charge. The current popularity of "design-build" contracting has allowed architects, in his opinion, to shirk "the responsibility they used to have in a 'traditional' practice." He says, "The engineer was pushed out and had to find new markets. Also, demanding clients armed with MBAs, but less sensitive to the built environment, began to participate in the process to watch the bottom line more closely."

"The traditional team approach built up over decades flourished until a number of years ago," notes consulting engineer Lois Roberts of Westport, CT. "The architect understood consulting engineers enough to make it work — and vice versa. Then the team started to unbundle. Engineers claim that architects who were the leads abandoned their responsibility to others on the team, so engineers went after jobs on their own to strike better deals."

QUALITY OR LOW BID

Whatever happened, engineers continue to complain that architects, as lead or prime designers, land their jobs via the preferred qualifications-based selection (QBS) method, then select subconsultants (usually consulting engineers) by low bid. To the engineer's way of thinking, this defeats the purpose of supporting QBS, endorsed by both professions, as a means of delivering top-quality design and performance. Both professions suffer as long as the public perceives that architects and engineers are adversaries embroiled in petty bickering.

While both professions are guilty of turf-guarding and ego-stretching practices, "the real problem is that everyone is semi-responsible," observes Philadelphia architect Susan Maxman who, in 1993, served as AIA's first woman president. "It starts with our education. In architecture schools, we're *not* trained to think about collaboration with other disciplines." Adding that engineers, too, have been "brainwashed into inflexibility," Maxman suggests that engineering schools should strive to make its students more aware of architectural considerations. "We need to better understand each other's values," she adds.

What's the difference between architects and consulting engineers anyway? Many engineers admit they perceive architects as problem finders and engineers as problem solvers. Engineers, they feel, tend to be linear thinkers who run things more like a business while architects are more devoted to their art...and that description frustrates both of them. "Vive le difference!" some might say — we should point to the strengths of each discipline. But the analogy brings us back to the earlier question: Who should be the prime designer and lead the design team? The business person or the artistic person?

"Design lead depends on the project and the contractual arrangement," Maxman points out. "I do feel the architect is the one who should lead the team in a largely architectural project. We are the generalists who have to coordinate and balance every part of the project — landscape architects, mechanical engineer, electrical and structural. But if the architect and engineer are doing their jobs in balance, you'll have a well-coordinated, beautiful project."

Echoing Maxman's sentiments, Paoluccio supports the architect as lead on public buildings that are "high-profile architecturally." On most other types, it could be either. And when engineers are the lead, he suggests we change the term "consulting engineers" to "prime engineers" responsible for representing the owner and hiring the architect. "The larger firms are doing that almost exclusively and they see no barriers at all," he adds.

GRAY AREAS

Of course, legal requirements also can determine who takes the lead. Yet, many projects have "gray" areas that make it difficult to distinguish between "engineering-heavy" and "architectural-heavy." Such situations exacerbate disagreements between architects and engineers. In most cases, "engineers practice within a single discipline," argues Philadelphia architect Paul Bott, in contrast, architects are trained to view design from a much broader perspective, looking at and integrating all the disciplines into the whole.

Yet, value-engineering studies suggest that more consulting engineers should be the prime designers, or at least play a more prominent role on the architect's team. Increased use of the professional who designed the building's structural, electrical or mechanical systems during construction — to see those systems are built as designed — would decrease the likelihood of litigation.

To build successful teamwork that results in higher quality buildings and more satisfied clients, owners and users, both professions must resolve their tiffs, reach out to each other and jump on the partnering bandwagon. Through partnering, architects and engineers can share ideas better, improve communications, and grow stronger together technically, professionally and personally.

In recent years, many A/Es have made significant strides toward attaining mutual respect and understanding. Yet, a considerable number of architects still believe they must always head up all design teams. They find nothing wrong with selecting their engineering consultants by low bid. Some even maintain their seal should be the only one valid on the drawings and necessary for getting a building permit. For obvious reasons, most engineers do not agree. They find this attitude harmful to the concept of teamwork. Even more important, they feel it does not serve the best interests of the client or the building users, since it creates a potential adversarial situation from the "get go."

ENGINEERS CONTRACTING WITH OWNERS

For a number of years, a trend in the U.S. and worldwide shows an increasing number of consulting engineers contracting directly with owners rather than architects on people-space buildings. These engineers indicate they are doing this for several reasons. In addition to the reluctance of being selected by low-ball bidding, the main ones are:

- The increased importance (and magnitude) of engineering — and engineering systems — in certain building types.
- Management tactics used by architects, such as slow payment of the engineer's fee — keeping and using the consultant's money long after the owner has paid the architect.
- Unrealistic budgets and schedules, and the resistance of using consulting engineers to observe construction of the systems they designed.
- Reluctance to credit the contributions of consultants when a project's uniqueness may be an engineering feat.

These complaints from engineers about architects as prime designers do not go unanswered. Architects have criticisms of engineers as members of the design team as well. Many believe engineers lack design sensitivity, are inflexible, can't articulate designs and offer little help in obtaining the project's design commission.

These sets of complaints should not be what dismantles any traditionally successful working relationships A/Es have had. They are serious concerns, of course, and not all of them will ever fully be taken care of to everyone's complete satisfaction. But we must find ways, as partners, to make the A/E team as strong as possible.

It's important to understand that many forces outside our professions — political, social, economic, demographic — will shape the future of architecture and engineering. For example, we are seeing an ever-increasing number of design-build projects. Often neither architects nor engineers are included as part of top management team — where major decisions affecting design are being made. In more cases than not, the team leader is a construction contractor or construction manager. Additionally, in some new project delivery systems and public-private undertakings, the prime design leader is even a non-construction industry type; he or she is a financial wizard, an accountant, a lawyer or some other profession.

MULTI-DISCIPLINARY DESIGN TEAMS

Today's design community is not just made up of architectural firms and engineering firms. A big part of that community includes complex and multi-disciplinary design firms, some quite large in size. In addition to engineers and architects, many design teams include social scientists, environmentalists or economists, according to Albert Dorman, chairman of the architecture/engineering firm Daniel, Mann, Johnson and Mendenhall (DMJM) in Los Angeles.

About the debate on what discipline — engineer or architect — should head up and manage the design team, Dorman maintains that a project manager's professional discipline is not important. "If you are a good project manager, independent, with the ability to lead a team and make a project succeed, then you should do it, no matter what your professional discipline," he stresses. (Dorman is a Fellow of both AIA, ACEC and an Honorary Life Member of the American Society of Civil Engineers.)

INDUSTRY-WIDE PARTNERING

The success of built-environment construction is not solely dependent on designers and partnering by engineers and architects. The team is much bigger than that and, according to Widom and AIA, the whole owner-contractor-architect-engineer relationship needs to be scrutinized. Observing that collaborative leadership not only applies to A/Es, Widom says, "it works equally well in our relationship with our partners in the construction industry. He suggests we "must develop and nurture the concept of partnership among the design professionals, the contractors, and all those other entities that are so much a part of what we do today and what we will be doing tomorrow."

Design professionals can play active roles in seeing that teamwork spreads beyond the design phase into the building phases — construction and maintenance. The benefits are clear: projects will be completed on time, within budget, to high standards and the satisfaction of everyone. "Owners are tired of hearing architects and engineers and contractors blame each other," offers Walter Moore (the Thomas Bulloch Chair and professor in charge of Texas A&M's Center for Building Design & Construction). Partnering fixes the problem.

PROJECT PARTNERING

Many engineering groups, echoing the U.S. Corps of Engineer's position on the matter, endorse and support partnering for the design and construction of built-environment projects. Both AIA and ACEC strongly believe, however, that, for it to be successful, partnering must begin with the use of QBS both for the selection of the prime designer *and* for the selection of subconsultants by the prime. Lawler cautions A/Es, "As we beat the drums for QBS, we must make sure our team members are well qualified." He adds, "When working with contractors, we must explain the scope of work well — so we must pick design team members with the quality and training to do the job."

AIA and ACEC further believe that:

- Partnering is a cooperative relationship between the providers and recipients of a product in which a "team attitude" is established and a successful outcome is achieved.
- Partnering does not establish or replace the legal or contractual relationship between the provider and recipient of products and services.
- Partnering is a way of doing business that enhances the desired project result within the legal or contractual relationship.

Three key ingredients are necessary for successful partnering:

- A positive attitude that promotes commitment, trust, understanding, and excellence
- Preparation that establishes clear expectations and mutual goals and objectives
- Perseverance, in which partners commit to execution, responsiveness, open communication and feedback

This requires that partnering participants must:

- Undertake early preparation and education.
- Secure management commitment.
- Conduct a joint pre-project workshop (or retreat) to create a partnering charter.

- Establish regular, open communication.
- Conduct final evaluation and reach project closure.

Partnering holds great promise for preventing disputes. However, because a partnering relationship is "extra-contractual," it cannot deal with risk allocation. All partners in a relationship must understand that agreements reached on a particular project relate only to that project. Conscious efforts must be made to involve all stakeholders, even if it complicates the interaction and the protocols established to manage it. Another important caveat: attitude is key to partnering.

TEAM RAPPORT

The practice of partnering has emerged as a extremely useful project administration concept because it restores the team rapport needed to deliver a project on time, within or below cost, at intended quality levels and free of unresolved claims. According to Phoenix consulting engineer Ronald Ewing, past chair of ACEC's Quality Management Committee, "Overall partnering reinstates the respect, flexibility and open communications that characterized so much of the construction industry before the era of litigation," He adds, "It may yet become the building industry's cornerstone for a reincarnation of traditional values."

Partnering (or managing problems together) is based on the concept that disputes stem from confrontational relationships. It is essentially a project-specific business plan incorporating a process of constant improvement, problem solving (before the attorneys) and team building, explains Tom Brasher of the Effectiveness Institute.

Five major ingredients (or players) are needed, he suggests, for successful partnering: leaders, champions, volunteers, fringe players and facilitators. Applied from top to bottom, this management/communications process addresses all the issues with all the players right from the start. In addition to reducing paperwork, partnering means faster delivery, fewer arguments and greater rewards.

Paul Sprehe, the former director of mechanical and electrical engineering at HTB, Inc., Oklahoma City, and a past president of ACEC, summarizes it this way: "It is a form of teamwork in which all members, although diverse in their viewpoints, agree in their roles to give their best efforts to complete a project successfully for the user, who should also be a team member." He goes on, "The process is not meant to subvert the interest of individual partners but to retain integrity and promote individual efforts."

This brings up a potential downside to partnering, Sprehe points out. Some members might see it as a threat to their leadership, forcing them to relinquish their role in a construction project.

"It's a matter of someone's ego being stronger than the good of all," he adds. "Sometimes the leader of a big firm is used to being the big boss at all times. Partnering doesn't work unless all major players — the architect, engineer, general contractor, construction manager, key subcontractors, consultants, client, user — buy into it."

"After all," he notes, "one bad apple can spoil a bushel." (More on this later in the Gorillas Section.) Other than bruised-ego problems, partnering has no economic, professional or liability disadvantages, says Sprehe.

A small federal project at the HTB-designed Oklahoma City Airport succeeded, Sprehe says, "because all partners — including the owner — were bought into the team process. They underwent training together, managed the project carefully and maintained communication lines. When it was all over, they shook hands bearing no grudges and having no loose ends."

TREND INTO THE NEXT CENTURY

"Arguably, partnering is the hottest construction industry trend of the 1990s," says McGraw-Hill's new book, *Partnering in Design and Construction.* In its introduction, co-author Kneeland Godfrey, Jr. of the Institute of Management and Administration (IOMA) explained that partnering can refer to many different relationships, including single-project partnering; multi-project, strategic partnering between a contractor (or prime designer) and a client; several non-traditional approaches of the "we are a family" idea at the heart of partnering.

"Partnering between contractors and private clients is as old as construction itself," Godfrey noted. The 100-year-old Cincinnati construction firm Al Neyer attributes its success in single-project partnering to its "client-first" attitude, according to president Don Neyer. "If you serve your clients' best interests, you'll create friends. They'll come back to you when they need to build."

When single-project partnering with public clients first started, construction chief Dan Burns of the Corps of Engineers recalls, "We wanted to clear the (emotional, human-relations) decks so project problems can be addressed." If the Corps could transform each person from an individual to a member of the team, he noted, "it stood to benefit from...better answers, less defensiveness." Burns adds that partnering can make work more satisfying. "Before, if there was a problem, a person would say, 'I've got a problem — got to solve it myself.' Today, if anyone on the team has a problem, it's everyone's problem."

SUCCESSFUL PROJECTS

Outstanding success stories are being added to the record books at a steady and encouraging pace. Constant case histories illustrate various ways of partnering. None is more notable than the one-half-billion-dollar section of I-70 through Glenwood Canyon in Colorado. It includes not only the partnering efforts of the designers and builders — the Colorado Department of Transportation (CDOT), several consulting engineering firms and construction companies — but with citizens groups and environmentalists.

For a project of such massive scale to be so successfully built through such a intricate and environmentally sensitive section of nature with almost universal public support is a tribute to the men and women who teamed together and got it done. (Basically completed in the mid-1990s at a cost of $450 million, it would cost well over $600 million if constructed today.)

In his book on the undertaking, *Wooing a Harsh Mistress*, John Haley, a consulting engineer heavily involved with the design work, recounts "not merely how a super-highway fused the competing claims of technology, esthetics and nature, but how the canyon herself exacted heavy concessions from the designers and builders of I-70."

In a smaller example, a $4-million Bonneville Lock project on the Columbia River was built successfully only because of partnering. According to Godfrey, the project's main subcontractor Donald B. Murphy of Federal Way, WA, admitted that partnering on this job not only saved his company but changed his attitude toward future work and business. Murphy claimed its partnering attitude — successful negotiations and early payment of equitable adjustments — "paid off at the bottom line."

Another case study, again from Godfrey, shows how a contractor once labeled a "claims contractor" was converted to partnering. After filing dozens of claims on a Corps of Engineers waste-water job at Fort Dix, NJ, MCI Construction of Woodbridge, VA, was terminated for convenience by the owner. Subsequently, MCI 's president, Clement Mitchell met with Col. Richard Sliwoski of the Corps. They agreed to start anew and give partnering a try — to work together as a cohesive team to produce a quality project. MCI's business approach was transformed from confrontational to one based on partnering. The project was a big success: completed in accordance with the contract, on time, within budget and at a fair profit for the contractor.

Denver architect James Bradburn (CW Fentress JH Bradburn Architects, PC) describes how partnering transformed the construction of Washington state's Natural Resources Agencies Building in Olympia into a winner.

"The project had reached a point where all parties — the owner, the constructor and the architect — felt disenfranchised from the process and powerless," he said. "The constructor was claiming he was incurring extra costs for which he wanted reimbursement. The owner felt the economic value of the project was declining due to threatened claims. The architects felt powerless to force the contractor to respect the design intent. Then we tried partnering.

"The results were spectacular," recalls Bradburn. "After the initial sessions and buy-ins, communications returned, solutions (rather than defensive posturing) were promoted, and the sticky issues of cost overruns, budget, schedule and maintaining design intent were solved to mutual satisfaction.

"The process was hard," he continues. "It required strong commitments by all the parties and reinforced the need for the designers to take a strong and useful role in solving construction-related problems." Today, the Natural Resources Agency Building is an award-winning building, viewed with pride by all the participants and the public.

On a $9.6-million city sewage-plant upgrade in the Dallas suburb of Garland, TX, general contractor Martin K. Eby Construction Company of Fort Worth was able to finish the 18-

month job in 15 months — a 16 percent time savings. The early completion resulted largely because the three key parties — the contractor (Eby), the owner (the city of Garland), and the engineer (Black & Veatch) — had become teammates.

Partnering also improves construction safety. For example, on the construction of a large sewage treatment plant addition in Clark County, NV, the owner-contractor-engineer team exceeded its extremely aggressive safety goals by having 300,000 hours of field labor with zero lost-time accidents.

When the Associated General Contractors (AGC) awarded its first Marvin M. Black Excellence in Partnering Awards in 1993, the eight recipients were asked: "How can partnering be improved on your next project?" They relied almost unanimously, "Be more inclusive." They also suggested partnering be started early — at the beginning of the design process — and "always invite key subcontractors, superintendents, foremen and rank-and-file coworkers to participate."

Partnering early on with its consulting engineers has paid off for Susan Maxman Architects. Although the small firm has no formal team-building process, explains Maxman. "We keep an open attitude — it's just the way we work! Getting input from engineers right from the start — even before the onset — is incredibly useful and creates a smoother process."

On a recent $14 million renovation project — an academic/dormitory complex at Kutztown (Pennsylvania) State University — Maxman's firm had an extremely tight schedule. It pulled in its engineers at the very beginning of the design process. By using CAD (computer-aided drafting and design) while working closely with its engineers, the architects were able to weave an all-new, energy-efficient system into a late-19th-century structure "without intruding on its historic character." The mechanical and electrical engineers were instrumental in figuring out, early on, a "very difficult" fire-protection, heating and cooling system. "Working together as a team produced great results," she adds. "It allowed construction to stay on schedule and within budget."

PARTNERING WITH GORILLAS

As Lois Roberts points out, "The way our projects are actually designed and built, the participants are not really equal — in most cases they are not even close." She adds, "Inequalities abound in major ways such as access to the client (owner), access to information, ability to understand risk and being in a prime position to negotiate fees. The prime position is the most powerful position on the design team because it is the closest to the owner (the money). Rarely do the owner-to-prime privileges — not insignificant in my experience — extend past the first tier.

She continues, "If architects and engineers, who are primes, really want to partner in the true sense, they must model it to protect the most vulnerable subs on the project even at the expense of themselves. By doing this, the prime is giving up its rights not only to advantages implied in a traditional team, but also to shared rights implied in 'partnering', and taking one of the seats in the back of the bus with everybody else. Hard to consider, harder even to do but, for design teams trying to build trust, it's a good place to start."

Roberts' comments concerning certain difficulties with partnering (and why it sometimes does not work) are well founded. Partnering, indeed, can be similar to the law of the jungle: if there is a gorilla or two on the team and they want to control, the process accomplishes little. A partnering arrangement controlled and manipulated by gorillas — usually those with the money (owners) or the prime designer or construction contractor — often proves to be a sham. Partnering is only given lip service and no one really benefits, not even the gorillas.

If, on the other hand, sound partnering principles are followed by all key players from the owner down to subconsultants (no matter the size of their fee or contract) — without concern for "having control" or taking care of "number one" — it creates an atmosphere for the most successful project. Adhering to critical schedules, providing necessary input, understanding why each participant is a key partner and being dedicated to achieving the most in quality and life-cycle engineering for the agreed upon dollar value is critical. Above all, honesty among partners is essential.

In a way, it might seem the most powerful people at the "top of the food chain" need to be magnanimous or altruistic. But today's construction project is a highly complex, team-oriented venture built with special-interest groups and public watchdogs scrutinizing every detail. To only be concerned with one's self interest proves to be short sighted and counter productive. Just saying you are partnering is not the answer; *true* partnering is.

NEW STANDARDS OF EXCELLENCE

By reducing fences and blending our know-how, creativity and talent, engineers, architects and builders can function in partnerships that consistently satisfy client expectations, schedules and budgets. Through cooperation, mutual respect and a shared commitment to sound problem solving, today's design and construction teams can chart new standards of excellence for the professions.

Nothing comes easy, of course, but as the world develops quickly to meet the new, technological future of the 21st century, everyone in the design and build professions needs to play our part in making it work. Though we are often independent and head-strong, the challenges ahead in the built-environment arena demand teamwork and collaboration.

13

TOMORROW'S ENGINEER

*"The highest reward for a person's toil is not what
they get for it, but what they become by it."*

—John Ruskin

Today's high school and college students will become this
country's leaders — and the world's as well — in the first part
of the next millennium. Those that have chosen to be engineers
will definitely be in the heat of the battle on issues concerning
American productivity, the environment and sustainable
development, and our quality of life. It is increasingly clear
that science and technology will advance more over the next
few decades than in all recorded history. The skills of our engineers — and, indeed, the scientific and technological literacy of
our general populace — will be put to the test.

The following is the address I gave at a recent banquet
honoring the graduating class from the College of Engineering at the University of Colorado at Denver (UCD). I urged
them to reflect on the significance of the profession they had
chosen and its impact on the world at large — and their probable role as leaders in it.

In the audience, in addition to the graduates themselves and their families, were undergraduates as well as engineering leaders from industry. Because it is a metro-city institution, most of UCD's students are older and more serious than the traditional college student. Many earn their degrees while holding full-time jobs — sometimes as para-engineers — and are more tuned in than younger students to the realities of business, life and the world around them.

This talk encapsulates most of the ideas presented in this book. In a way, the address is a compendium of all the book's essays, and all the issues facing engineers and our profession. Because it is such, it draws on some of the words and phrases put forth in earlier chapters. Hopefully the reader will find any repetition purposeful, not distracting.

Here is the address in its entirety.

TOMORROW'S ENGINEER

Before I begin, I want to thank Dean (Peter) Jenkins for the invitation to address you tonight and to talk about, among other things, two of my favorite subjects: the importance of this great and noble profession to civilization, and the contributions engineers can make if we take on leadership roles in society.

It is hard to believe that year 2000 is staring us right in the face. I'm sure you'll all agree that there will be lots of changes on the horizon. When I was a boy growing up on the high plains of northeastern Colorado, I was a big fan of Buck Rogers — space explorer of the comic books — and to me year 2000 was like the exploits of ole Buck, so far away — so far out there — I never thought I would be around to see the day. And I never thought any of the space travel tales the science fiction writers were concocting would ever really materialize.

Well, I was certainly wrong on the latter, and hopefully, if my health stays as good as it is, I will be wrong about the former and will live, along with most of you, well into the next century.

We have been to the moon; communication satellites are commonplace as is the use of FAX to convey information. Soon even that will be replaced by the Internet. The uses for virtual reality techniques, likewise, are limitless — the new Boeing 777 aircraft, now in our skyways, is an example. It will be the first commercial plane designed and tested using simulation. And these are only a few of the latest significant engineered products and systems. Many more will continue to arrive on the scene, at an ever-increasing rate, and you will be in the middle of it all. How exciting! What a challenge! I only wish my career were just starting!

And technical and engineering challenges are not the only ones tomorrow's engineer will encounter. Tomorrow's engineer will face many other major and exciting challenges, requiring solutions only they can provide. Actually, all of us throughout our lives will always face many choices that will affect our lives and careers. And we must be prepared for these. As that sage, old baseball philosopher Yogi Berra, has often been quoted as saying, "When you come to a fork in the road, take it."

The fork in the road I want to challenge you with tonight is the leadership fork. I want to challenge each of you to look at the bigger picture of things and consider the impact you as an engineer can have on the world around you by becoming a leader not only in engineering but in society as well.

Many notable Americans call engineers the wealth creators — former Colorado governor Dick Lamm and Andrew Young, former ambassador to the United Nations, are among them. They suggest that engineers are not pie-dividers but are the ones capable of increasing the pie of opportunity for all.

Industry leaders like Lee Iacocca (of Chrysler fame) and Jack Welch (CEO of General Electric) are loud and clear — and outspoken — in their claim that this nation's economic well being, in the future, will depend on its engineers.

Welch reminds us that without its engineers, Japan would never have become the global economic powerhouse it is today. In Japan, 70 percent of their industries' upper management are engineers, while in the U.S., it is only 30 percent. Tomorrow's engineer can change this. For America to maintain its economic position in the world, it will need to continue to rely on its engineers.

Engineers take an idea and turn it into reality — a computer chip, for instance, into a machine that does something. Without engineers, most of the discoveries of modern science would remain laboratory curiosities. The laser is an example; Einstein and his buddies knew about it for years but it took an engineer to develop the first usable laser beam, which he did using a bar of ruby.

Engineers always come up with the real solutions: how to build a spectacular bridge; how to purify the air and water; how to design a useful product like an automobile or a spacecraft; how to plan intelligent buildings; how to turn wind into energy or sunlight into electricity. Engineering know-how was behind the technical success of the recently completed tunnel under the English Channel (physically linking England for the first time with the rest of Europe). Many call the $18 billion venture "the greatest construction project of the century," taking the honor away from our own Interstate Highway System — another venture highly dependent on innovative engineering.

The world is becoming so much more technically dependent and sophisticated — young children in the first grade are using computers on a daily basis, and they are whizzes at it. I thought it was a big deal when I learned to use a slide rule when I was a college freshman in the mid-fifties.

As tomorrow's engineers, those of you who are graduating (or who are just beginning your careers in engineering) are in for some real exciting times. You will be the intellectual mainstream of the greatest creative time in human history. And because of this, tomorrow's engineer, the matchless problem solver, will more and more be in the forefront and needed in leadership roles. You will have much opportunity to impact many lives.

Just the word: engineering — to engineer — has a ring to it, an excitement.

Whenever some star quarterback like Denver's John Elway or Green Bay's Brett Favre brings their team from a sure defeat to a victory in the last seconds of a game, the sports writers say he *engineered* a miracle — he did something masterful (produced a skillful winning drive).

Engineers likewise are masterful producers. They get things done in the most skillful ways, which is why we have the reputation of being wealth creators and the ones to call on where there are complex problems to solve. We are also known as the designers of our nation's infrastructure, the protectors of our environment — the maintainers, if you will, of everyone's very standard of living.

You are joining a profession that has in its ranks more than 10 million members worldwide (more than 2 million of them are here in the U.S. alone). What an awesome potential for power and getting things accomplished. Engineers, it seems, are everywhere, doing a mind-boggling array of intriguing things. They are employed in small and large companies, in countless industries and with governmental agencies. Around 60 percent work in industry, 20 percent in the government, 5 percent in construction, 5 percent in academia and 10 percent in private practice as consultants (which is my field).

Dean Jenkins asked if I would share with you how I came to be a consulting engineer and describe some of my firm's work. To begin: the roads leading to a career as a consulting engineer are as varied as are the types of engineers. There are consultants in nearly all the main fields of engineering: mechanical, electrical, civil, structural, industrial, acoustical, environmental, software —- and the list goes on.

I got into consulting engineering in a fairly direct way. Math and science were always fairly easy subjects and I liked building things. My father was a general contractor, and I worked for him summers since I was in junior high school. My father is an outstanding man and a fine role model, and I've always admired him and his work. And I remember whenever the engineers came out to the construction site — of a bridge or a big structure of some sort — they always had the right solutions, could answer all my father's questions...and they seemed to boss my father around. As a boy, I thought, wow, if these guys can boss my dad around they must be really, really important people. I want to become one of them! So when I came of age, off I went to college to become an engineer — a big, smart and important engineer.

After four years of cramming in five years of course work to get a four-year bachelor of science degree — as most of you have done — I graduated from college. I immediately went, with high hopes and big plans, to work for the U.S. Bureau of Reclamation to design those enormous dams and power plants.

Well, my first assignment was to design a small septic tank for a small government construction camp! After the first shock of it all wore off, and with most of the air out of my balloon, I set out to design the best septic tank the world had ever before seen. I wanted to do such a good job, I even took my assignment home with me at night to work on it — I never could get myself around to telling my young bride (who was so proud of me) what I was working on. I worked and worked on my tank design, using all the formulas and the latest, greatest design techniques I had learned in school.

Finally, after about two weeks of this, the supervisor of my supervisor — the big man, the head of the department — stopped by to check on my progress. I could tell from the look on his face that my reams and reams of calculations where not impressing him. He then told me I was making too big of a deal out of it — that the Bureau had standard designs for septic tanks and all they wanted me to do was pick one out of the tables, and get on to another assignment. I learned an embarrassing (and never to be forgotten) lesson that day about the importance of communicating and understanding what is expected. My immediate supervisor and I, from that day forward, were never what you would call "close."

I guess I was like most engineering graduates of my day. I took a lot of technical courses, which helped me learn my "craft" (as they say), but I took virtually no courses in communications.

When asked what college courses benefited them most in their careers, nearly all engineering leaders in our industry tell us this: in the first years out of school, technical courses are most needed; ten years later, it's management, economics and product costing; 15 to 20 years after graduation, they say "Shakespeare" — and the humanities, public speaking and interaction with others. Most wish they had been more broadly educated. The two most important skills they have used throughout their careers are teamwork (team building) and communications.

All of us spend 50 percent of our waking hours in communication - reading, writing, talking, listening. Communications is probably the most important skill in life. I hope all of you will make it a lifetime goal to become the very best you can at it. I know it will be an immeasurably helpful tool for you in advancing up the rungs of the ladder of success.

Well, after four years with the government, I was still married to the same woman (I had yet to tell her about my septic tank design ordeal), had two kids, a newly acquired masters degree and my professional registration as a licensed engineer. I was ready for something new. I took a 20 percent cut in pay and went to work for a local Denver consulting engineering firm, a very good firm, and worked on some terrific projects: the Currigan Convention Center and several high-rises.

By now I was hooked, I knew which fork in the road I would take. Yogi Berra would have been real proud of me. It's now been over 30 years since I founded my own company (gone into private practice) and I've never had a dull moment. Confucius (or some other wise, old philosopher, maybe Yogi) said, "Choose a job you love and you will never have to work a day in your life." Well, consulting engineering has been like that for me.

My firm has designed projects all over the world and throughout this country including a hotel for the Summer Olympics in South Korea, the tallest office building in Jeddah, Saudi Arabia, industrial plants in Russia and parking structures in major cities like Chicago, Kansas City and L.A. Locally we've completed countless projects, big and small: buildings, bridges and roadways. Many were award winners, like the Jefferson County Courthouse and the I-70 (Chambers Road) Bridge — the most frequently driven *under* bridge on the interstate going to the new Denver International Airport (DIA). We engineered all three of the concourse structures at DIA (but let me stress, we had nothing to do with the baggage systems).

We even once did a project for Jimmy and Tammy Bakker, an amusement park in North Carolina similar to the new Elitch's Park here in Denver. The thing I remember most about Jimmy and Tammy's project is that he didn't want to pay us the last 10 percent of our fee because he had a dream where, as he told it, the Lord wanted him to sue someone, either the contractor or the engineer. Lucky for us, a dream a couple of nights later turned out in our favor because the Lord, according to what was told us, clarified for the Rev. Bakker that he was to sue the contractor. We were paid in full and never went back for any more work with the Bakkers.

As rewarding as my field is and will be in the future, it is not without its problems — putting the Bakker-type aside for the moment. Many of the basic problems for consulting engineers are similar to those for all fields of engineering, and cannot be solved or even properly addressed just within the narrow confines of the engineering industry. For as long as I can remember, whenever groups of engineers gather, conversation always comes around to our image and why we don't get more respect. Whenever consultants gather, discussions — after we tire of talking about our poor image — usually gravitate to three additional concerns: selection by low fee rather than qualifications; frivolous lawsuits (inhibiting creativeness), excessive government regulations (and unfair competition with the private sector).

The problem in the past has been that we engineers have been "talking amongst ourselves." It is evident that our dilemmas will not be resolved by keeping them within the confines of our engineering meetings. Now is the time for us engineers as professionals to boldly step up to the plate and take the "quantum leap" to the next level. To get involved in the world outside of engineering, telling the public how what we do impacts their daily lives. This is the state of the industry you new and recent graduates are entering.

To adequately address the dilemmas facing engineers, all engineers, young and old, need to get involved in the broader community, the one that deals with "big-picture" issues and public policy making. More engineers, in the future, must become leaders in society to better control their own destiny and impact public direction. Tomorrow's engineer will need to hone his or her natural leadership and communications skills and sit at the table where decisions are made — decisions affecting his or her livelihood. Those, and not the closed, tight-knit engineering meetings, are the forums where we will get things done to correct the issues affecting us, and control our own professional futures.

As you progress in your career as an engineer, you will, definitely, at some point have two significant forks in the road to chose between: being a specialist, a technical expert only — or generalist, a manager or leader of others. And that is what is so great about a career in engineering. You have so many options and things you can do.

Whichever direction you take, as a member of a respected profession, you have a responsibility to be a good citizen. For an engineer to say he or she does not want to get involved in community or civic affairs because he or she is an introvert or not good at communicating is a cop out. We are a learned profession just like law and medicine, and we must contribute to society. We are duty bound to participate in our communities. It should be one of our first and foremost concerns.

Because we are creative and can solve the most difficult of problems, and are the ones educated to be dealing with advancing technologies, we need to speak out on issues. We have great potential for being the heroes and the leaders in molding tomorrow's world. But we must be outspoken on technological matters the world is undergoing to be considered as leaders. It is alarming, for instance, that the legal profession and not engineers (or scientists) have often taken the lead in addressing the "greenhouse effect" (global warming) or sustainable development.

Tomorrow's engineer must be pro-active and must get involved in writing and talking in public forums about how technology affects everyone, all facets of people's lives (their standards of living). We must do what we can to make technology and engineering relevant to the layperson, especially to school-age children.

And just because you are now college graduates, it does

not mean your learning days are over. They never are. It is said that our technical knowledge has a life of around seven years, then it is obsolete. To stay current and at the leading edge of your profession, you must dedicate yourself to lifetime learning. That might not be what you wanted to hear right now, but sleep on it.

I have always considered myself very fortunate to have been able to become an engineer. Being an engineer has such a spirit of adventure to it. You get to design things — products and structures and systems — and you get to see them get built....and, with a true sense of pride, watch them be used.

Remember that movie "It's a Wonderful Life"? They show it about a hundred times every holiday season (from Thanksgiving to Christmas). The hero of the saga, Jimmy Stewart as George Bailey, has this dream to be a civil engineer, design big, important projects all over the world. Throughout the movie he has this dream to do these things and travel the world. Something always comes up and he never leaves Bedford Falls. He was never able to live his dream — to become an engineer.

Many of my colleagues here tonight and I myself have been able to live that dream, to become an engineer and do exciting projects all over the world. Many of you will too. Engineering is a noble calling with many opportunities for all of you, whether you go into consulting or industry or any of the many other fields of practice.

Keep in mind, however, that just doing great in engineering may not be enough. Many of you will be called upon, and will become industry's leaders and society's leaders. Being wealth creators and protectors of everyone's standard of life, in and of itself, will be most rewarding. But for those of you who become leaders, it may be even more exhilarating. However, it will demand that you not only be a technical expert, but also well-rounded in many subjects. It's wise to remember that technical competency does not translate into having sound judgment. That comes with having a "big picture" perspective. How can you prepare for leadership? Here are my thoughts on the subject:

The "Six Steps to Leadership Plan." It is a plan for personal development to prepare us for those forks in the road that we will encounter during our careers. The plan should occur parallel with the continued development of your technical and job-required skills. It is pertinent to not only those of you who are graduating today, but all engineers just starting out.

The beauty of it is that you can do each item at your own pace, and don't forget to take care of your family and personal life while you are advancing your career. Keep that part of your life rich and wholesome.

1. Continue education after graduation. (Take classes outside of your field — history, literature, geography, political science.)

2. Maximize communication skills. (Improve your writing, speech-making and presentation skills. It is a shame some great ideas never get accepted because they are presented so poorly.)

3. Become an expert at something outside engineering. (Even if it is just an expertise at fly fishing, broaden your perspective. I'm into western history and have written a book and several papers on early Colorado history.)

4. Become active in community affairs (chambers of commerce, service clubs, community groups — little league baseball or soccer, boy scouts, girl scouts, etc.).

5. Get involved in politics. (Serve on boards and commissions. To paraphrase Plato: "If intelligent people don't get involved in politics, they will soon find they are being ruled by the less intelligent.")

6. Find a mentor and/or role model, and this person doesn't necessarily have to be an engineer. (Study why they succeed.)

Those of you who are well into your careers are potential role models and mentors. The young engineers of today will be the leaders of tomorrow. You are in a powerful position to influence and impact what they will be as leaders. The young engineers of today will be the future leaders tomorrow and you can help them. Volunteer to assist and encourage them to reach their full potential.

We are just a couple of years away from the next century and the world around us is changing faster and faster every year. The need for engineers to solve the technological problems that will face us all is enormous. Tomorrow's engineer can mold the course of history and control his destiny if he will get more involved in solving "big picture" problems. The opportunities for tomorrow's engineer to be a leader are everywhere.

Society needs your talent and your problem-solving skills!

I'll close with these words of General Douglas MacArthur. He said: "There is no security on this earth; there is only opportunity."

Well, there is a lot of opportunity out there for tomorrow's engineers — now and into the future. I hope all of you go out there and fulfill your dreams — and become as rich and famous...and successful as you desire.

The future will be most fascinating and challenging. There will be some wonderful things to accomplish. And as you do, I hope you never take lightly that you are an engineer — improving and impacting many lives. Your potential for greatness is limitless.

Carpe diem — Seize the day!

Seize the moment....and take up the challenge to become the best there ever was in engineering, and to be society's leaders of the next millennium.

14

SEEING INTO THE FUTURE

*"Far and away the best prize that life offers is
the chance to work hard at work worth doing."*

—Theodore Roosevelt

There will always be a need for engineers, because there will always be many problems only we can solve. That issue is not high on my list of concerns. The biggest anxiety I have developed over the years is not that tomorrow's engineers will not have jobs or work to do. My concern is that engineers in the U.S. are more and more being treated as technicians rather than professionals — certainly not as professionals on par with lawyers and doctors. And my consternation is not just about whether engineering is a prestigious field or not, but about what effect the downgrading of it — of those that produce and add value — will have on the future American way of life.

Society and civilization cannot steadily progress and improve without its engineers, the builders who turn ideas into reality. This has been true since the first dawning of man and through the ages, and especially now that the world is so dependent on technology and its engineers.

ECONOMIC STABILITY

Emerging nations see technology as their entry into the modern world and economic stability. Strengthening their engineering industries is foremost on their agendas. In the summer of 1995, I was the U.S. representative to the United Nations Industrial Development Organization's (UNIDO's) first international summit on consulting engineering services in Vienna, Austria. There I had it strongly driven home to me how critical acquiring (and perfecting) a strong engineering base is to every country. Representatives of all the 30 or so emerging nations at the conference indicated their future economies were tied to increasing the capacity of their engineering industries.

UNIDO summarized their feelings by recording this statement: "The strategic significance of consulting engineering services in industrialization and economic development in industrialized countries is increasingly recognized." These engineering services "play a key role in industrial and economic development. They are the means by which project concepts are translated to industrial plants by successive application of knowledge and skills." They are pivotal catalysts in the "industrial and socio-economic development in developed and developing countries."

Norman Augustine, the 1995 chairman of the National Academy of Engineering, likewise states, "On a recent trip around the world, virtually every political leader I met indicated that science and technology formed the underpinning of their national strategy to improve the quality of life." These leaders, he stresses, "are committing their countries to high-tech futures. Yet, in this country, we seem to believe that science is best left to scientists.

"I am convinced that the lack of scientific (and the author would add engineering) understanding in this country is hurting us economically and socially," Augustine adds. "The majority of new jobs being generated here derive from technological advances. If those jobs are to stay here, we need a work force that is familiar and comfortable with the principles on which those jobs rest.

"The challenges we face as a nation are unprecedented in number and scope. If we hope to repair the environment, provide clean affordable energy, fuel economic growth and jobs, explore space, provide for our defense, improve health care, rebuild the nation's infrastructure, or address virtually any of the other problems we find in the modern world, we need a highly educated, science-minded work force. Setting high standards for all students in science is how we will create that work force."

Engineers as a group must step forward and lead the efforts to meet these national, "big picture" challenges. If we do not take on leadership roles to help shape the public agenda in the areas where we posses the skills and expertise, we will have failed in our responsibility as a learned profession. It will mean we have abdicated our rightful role in addressing the impacts of technology and engineering on the world leaving them to be dealt with by those less than qualified.

Before we go any farther with how we can step forward and chose the right forks to pursue, let us look at some of the more universal trends affecting society at large.

DEMOGRAPHICS AND TRENDS

There are several changing demographics that will impact tomorrow's engineers as well as society. The fabric of the workforce has been changing dramatically and will continue to do so. In most American families, both heads of the household have jobs. About 19 percent of today's engineering students are women, an eight-fold increase from 12 years ago. And while the current, typical engineer is an upper middle-class, white male, the American Society of Engineering Educators predicts that by 2025, this will change. The typical U.S. engineer will be "a foreign-born Asian woman who practices engineering as part of a dual income family."

Statistics on the employment of college graduates currently show that electrical engineering graduates, especially software engineers, are in extremely high demand. The placement office at the University of Colorado reports that, in the last couple of years, all their electrical engineering graduates, even the average students, have each received multiple job offers; some have even gotten signing bonuses a` la sports stars. Now that's the way young, budding engineers ought to be treated. The University of Colorado's experience is typical of many other leading engineering colleges. In most (not all but most) disciplines, there are currently more jobs than there are engineering graduates. The exception to that — where demand does not yet exceed supply — seems to be in fields like general civil and chemical engineering.

Early in the 21st century we will find that 80 percent of the world's population — six billion people — will be Asians, Latinos and Africans. Though reluctant in the past, more and more from the latter two groups are selecting engineering as a career path.

And Americans are aging. More than half of today's work force (in the U.S.) are nearly 50 years old. In two generations, it is predicted that 25 percent of the American population will be over 65 years of age, double what it is today.

These and other similar trends will influence the future of engineering. How we design elderly-people-friendly products and what standards we use for safety are two examples. The pressing national challenges pointed out throughout this book, many of which are elegantly summarized in Augustine's comments above, will also certainly be major issues. What are others?

Attempts to look into the crystal ball to see into the future usually end up with a series of dubious predictions, like the prediction that the production of edible lawns will someday soon become a profitable business venture. Some wise, old sage once said about forecasting, "There is only one thing for sure about the future. It will change."

I have always been personally amused by those who suggest they can predict the future. Most of the time, these forecasts miss the target completely. Very, very few, if any, professional futurists, for instance, predicted the coming down of the Berlin Wall. Instead, keep in mind what Winston Churchill said about crystal ball forcasts: "It is a mistake to look too far ahead. Only one link in the chain of destiny can be handled at a time."

So heeding that advice, I will not present a lot of distant predictions — many of which, like several in John Nasbitt's *Megatrends*, would probably prove to be wrong anyway. They only muddy the waters and distract from what I think are the real challenges facing the engineering profession. In any case, this book is not meant to be a forecaster of events. Its intent is to call engineers to action — to challenge us to become citizens of the world, to be leading-edge, world-class technical engineers so we can better impact what goes on around us — to open our eyes to all the possibilities, so we take the best forks in the road.

Any and all predictions hereafter mentioned deal with broad-stroke issues that lay the groundwork — identifying the future landscape, if you will — for the paths and roads we will face.

COMPUTERS AND INFORMATION

It does not take a rocket scientist (or rocket engineer!) to identify the two major technologies affecting everyone in a major way: information communication systems and computers.

What about computers of the future? After all, the world chess champion is now a computer, "Deep Blue," designed by IBM engineers.

Someday, computer-generated images may even replace actors and actresses in the movies and on television. Modern-day Walt Disneys may proliferate like rabbits. Much of the blockbuster movie "Jurassic Park" was computer generated, as were several scenes in "Forrest Gump." Is "virtual reality" as depicted in the movie "Disclosure" just around the corner? The new Boeing 777 — a fine machine — was the first commercial airplane designed by simulation and tested using virtual reality concepts. Will many other major products be brought forth in the same way in the coming days? I think so.

At our office — many of my colleagues in private practice report similar statistics — one engineer with a computer is doing what it took two engineers and a draftsman to do 15 years ago. And it's not just a labor issue. Computers let us do better designs and engineering because we can look at more options faster and in more depth than ever before.

What is really revolutionizing our operations, though, is the Internet and the exploding information technologies. How we get information and how we provide and transmit our work product to our clients and customers is changing overnight.

In my field (consulting engineering), global communication systems are becoming commonplace and national economies are being dramatically impacted in the process. We see more and more engineering assignments being done as a hybrid product: preliminary design done in the U.S., final engineering (drawings and specifications) done in South Korea and construction management by Europeans — all for a project in Malaysia. Often engineering work is being done on a 24-hour cycle; a firm in the U.S. works on the design for eight hours then sends it west for a team in the Pacific Rim. That company then forwards it (with their input) along to the next stop, in say, Germany.

There will be a time in the near future when we will all be talking to our laptops instead of punching our keyboards to input data.

The point should be clear: computer literacy is not just helpful; it is essential. Today, not tomorrow. And computer literacy demands that individuals and especially engineers (even us old guys) get up to speed on the latest technology now, then stay up to speed each and every day. What we experience now will most likely be obsolete and replaced with some new technique within a year, then again in half a year.

This isn't something we should scoff at or fight against as we did when the first vestiges of technology crept into our industry and our businesses. It is something we must embrace. The alternative is failure.

CREATIVITY

What major events or humankind needs will require attention in the next millennium? Here in the U.S. as well as most other countries, our infrastructure is aging (as was discussed in Chapter Seven). We have an impending infrastructure crisis that threatens our quality of life, our economic future, and the stability of the world.

On the international scene, global markets demand we be creative and produce sought-after products and services. We must be economically competitive. Ways need to be found to increase the world's economic pie — get it to grow — rather than merely divide it up more and more often.

How about other areas in which new technologies — engineering applications of technology — will play a significant role? Consider these:

- In the coming years, security systems and safeguards against terrorists will become even bigger concerns than they are now.
- Recreational and health care needs for an aging population need to be adequately thought out, as does our ever-increasing demand for prisons. Finding lasting solutions for both needs to go beyond just building more and more new facilities.
- Exploration of space and the oceans will be ongoing and astonishing.
- Mastering new technology and controlling the effects of bad technology to prevent disasters such as Chernobyl or the Challenger — and the Three Mile Island debacle — will be key challenges.
- Environmental concerns, such as clean water and air, and runaway waste, will require immense input from engineers. So will an increasing need for life-cycle engineering designing and costing, and solutions to sustainable development difficulties.

SUSTAINABLE DEVELOPMENT

Donald Roberts, former president of the World Engineering Partnership for Sustainable Development — an organization founded by the World Federation of Engineering Organizations (WFEO), an association that represents nearly ten million engineers worldwide — argues that the single most important initiative tomorrow's engineers must get involved with is "sustainable development." His group states: "The engineering community has a responsibility to take the concepts of sustainable development beyond rhetoric to action at the individual, corporate and institutional levels."

One of the key ingredients in attaining some form of sustainable equilibrium is what to do with the waste we produce. Hans-Peter Durr, an internationally recognized scientist says: "We should take an attitude that waste is not garbage. Waste is a resource in the wrong spot." Durr, former chairman of the Werner-Heisenberg Institute for Physics in Munich, Germany, explains, "The past was characterized by practically unlimited expansion. Whenever we ran short of resources, we invented substitutes. We didn't worry about generating and dumping waste because scientists and engineers would solve whatever problems the waste eventually caused."

He agrees with Roberts about the gravity of sustainable development, stating that we used to think all we had to do was "get the resources from nature and dump the waste back into nature, thinking it will work out.

"But we now have to make sure the cycle closes," he says. "It has become too big a job for nature. I think the future of science and engineering is to look at a product's whole life-cycle and not leave the task of disposal to nature. We should deliver a waste product that allows nature to close the cycle."

The concept of Sustainable Development (SD) was proposed by the United Nation's World Commission on Environment and Development in 1987. It instigated the 1992 world conference in Rio de Janeiro which brought together more than 120 heads of state to form a unified position on SD. It resulted in "Agenda 21," a 600-page summary of 2,500 sustainable development issues and recommended solutions. "The minimum costs to create a global sustainable future are estimated at $600 billion per year," reports James Poirot (the 1998 vice-president of WFEO and president of WFEO ComTech — the committee for transferring, sharing and assessment of technology).

The Commission's definition of sustainable development is: "Meeting the needs of the present without compromising the ability of future generations to meet their own needs."

Roberts says, "To me, a sustainable system as an engineer is one that is either in equilibrium, operating at a steady state, or a system which changes slowly, at a rate considered to be acceptable." He suggests *unsustainable* activities today are illustrated by the following facts:

- The population has increased by six times since the beginning of the industrial revolution (1790). It has tripled since 1900 and will double again within 40 to 50 years.
- In this century, global economic output has increased by a factor of 20, and the use of fossil fuels has increased by 30 times.
- Industrial production has increased by a factor of 100 times in 100 years and, as a result, 25 percent of the world's population in industrialized nations now consumes 80 percent of the world's goods.
- One billion people live on less than a dollar a day and 1.5 billion people do not have access to clean water.
- Forests are being destroyed at the rate of 100,000 square kilometers per year (an area the size of Indiana) and more than 5,000 species become extinct each year.

This increased consumption and the population growth has led to resource depletion and increased waste products. These in turn have led to environmental degradation. Global environmental problems are rapidly approaching a crisis and, for SD to be possible, something must be done soon to control these trends. Among other things, Roberts says, "Our human activities will have to be redesigned to reuse our raw materials and consumer products many times over.

"This will include salvaging construction materials such as concrete and asphalt, the reuse of metals and other natural and synthetic materials," he added. "Waste recycling and reuse will have to become a way of life."

Durr suggests, "Humans have to develop a lifestyle compatible with ecological sustainability, where everyone can live in equity without jeopardizing the health of our planet. This is a tremendous task, but I think it can be accomplished because I believe in the imagination of the human mind and that humans really care about the planet."

Poirot believes, "A sustainable world will evolve more rapidly when engineers commit to maintaining currency on sustainable technologies, when the U.S. president and foreign embassies have engineering advisors and when the UN consistently includes engineering views in their policies, agreements and operations. It must be accomplished through our initiative. We cannot be expected to be invited to the policy-making table out of our silent past."

Roberts feels that engineers have two choices to make in the future.

"We can remain as technical advisors to government agencies and clients or emerge as environmental leaders and decision makers," he said. "It's probably too late for most of us to make the choice as individuals. However, I think it would be possible to make a difference within one or two generations."

He proposes selectively recruiting gifted children to become environmental engineering leaders early, offering them full scholarships to obtain a broad engineering education, one "which combines the technical skills of engineering with a wide range of environmental disciplines. These studies would be integrated with a background in economics, law, history and literature, as well as the political sciences."

ENGINEERS AS THE HEROES?

Although leadership by engineers abounds in our industry and our profession has always been crucial to this nation's progress, few outside our ranks give our accomplishments much consideration. Our significant contributions basically remain behind closed doors, in the closet, if you will.

Many within our industry generally agree on the national challenges that our country (and the world) faces. The basic issues facing our profession that we (together with the public) must continue to address go hand in glove with these broader challenges. Delon Hampton, head of a national engineering firm based in Washington, D.C., mixes them together and suggests the most pressing are:

1. The engineer's image
2. Higher education
3. Our decaying infrastructure
4. International competition

Hampton reminds us that "the world's largest market for consulting engineering and construction services is the U.S., and our foreign competitors recognize it."

The desire of many in our industry to "attract the cream of the crop into engineering as a career" is an admirable goal, but one that Hampton suggested "will be largely unattainable if we do not take steps to improve the image of the engineer.

"It will also be increasingly difficult to attract the best and the brightest into engineering when last year (1991) the best and brightest law school graduates received starting salaries in the $85,000 range while business and finance were not far behind," he added. "Starting salaries for our top engineering students were substantially less." (The author reminds the reader that it takes a lot more schooling to get a law degree than it does to get a bachelor's degree in engineering.)

Money is not the only attraction — though it is a significant one — for young men or women when choosing a profession. The field has to have some heroes, role models worth looking up to, men and women who are doing meaningful things.

Who are our heroes and today's role models anyway? The media bombards us with celebrities constantly — mostly entertainers, many with dubious credentials and values. But surely celebrities without strong moral values are not the models needed in the long run.

Don't we need heroes with deep convictions and integrity, and solid work ethics who can produce and add value? Shouldn't many of our national role models come from the ranks of the producers and problem solvers? Don't engineers qualify? I believe large numbers of engineers across this country, with the right stuff, can be outstanding role models, not just for young engineers but for all American youth no matter what their calling. How do we identify them and bring them into the spotlight?

The exploits of countless engineers, especially those that are big-picture visionaries and community leaders, need to be brought into the limelight for all to see and admire. The accomplishments of outstanding personalities like Augustine, Jack Welch, Lee Iacocca, Gen. Hank Hatch and Sheila Widnall (the first woman to head a branch of the U.S. armed forces - Secretary of the Air Force) are wonderful examples of heroes and heroines for movies and books. (Because they all have a big picture perspective, I'll label them our "big-picture five" for future reference.)

Why aren't they household names? They say the greatest invention of modern society is the transistor. Who knows the inventor's name? Shouldn't that person's name be on the lips of every man, woman and child in America? Or high on the media's list of outstanding national heroes? (Actually three people shared the 1956 Nobel Prize for Physics for developing the transistor: William Shockley, John Bardeen and Walter Brattain).

Why aren't they and others like them well-known by the public? What they do (or have done) certainly impacts our lives. Why aren't they national heroes and role models? They are inspirational and noble figures, the positive role models the youth of today — tomorrow's leaders — need to study and emulate.

Hatch says many of our brightest and most talented young men and women do not chose engineering as a career because "it is not relevant to them." Building things, creating new products, improving everyone's standard of living and protecting the environment is not relevant?! For some reason, the message is not getting out there, informing people that engineering is exciting and that history-making is happening.

It is a real loss that the names of those changing the course of civilization — like the fathers of the transistor — remain unknown. Our young will never get to enjoy the excitement of their exploits. Whose fault is it that notables such as this remain anonymous? We engineers, I'm sad to say, are much to blame. We have been silent and invisible — overly shy and humble — much too long. Hopefully the time has come for us to correct this, to spring into action and do something about it.

ACTION

We need to do things that will attract more media and public attention. This, of course, means getting more active outside our industry. But consider other ways, too, not the least of which is starting at the grassroots level, getting involved with young people and making ourselves available as mentors.

Those of us well along in our careers must actively become role models as well as mentors, and not just to budding young engineers, but to all of our young people. Since we deal with the natural laws and the forces of this planet on a daily basis, it is natural we would show youngsters how to build things, taking these laws and forces into consideration.

To want to make something with our hands is a basic trait in all humans. And if you have ever shown a grade school child how to do just that — build something — recall their eagerness and enthusiasm. We must find a way to capture that moment and continue it with them for the rest of their lives — whether they become engineers or scientists or not. If they keep that sense of how exciting is was to be "engineers" for that brief moment in their youth, they as adults will be more apt to look upon practicing engineers in a totally different and favorable light — possibly as superstars. Who knows?!

MENTORING

Secretary Widnall believes that mentors are especially crucial to young females who want to be or have just become engineers. She says, "Most women scientists of my generation can point to a single individual without whose encouragement at the undergraduate level they would not have gone to graduate school." Additionally, she suggests ways to bridge the "age gap" now in her field, aeronautical engineering. Her comments apply to all fields.

This gap, Widnall points out, exists because "there is a large pool of aeronautical engineers who have retired or are close to retirement." On the other end of the spectrum, she says there is a pool of younger men and women who "are brilliant — facile with computers, and educated in the sciences. Their approaches to engineering, and their interests, differ from senior engineers." To keep the age gap from becoming a capability gap, she stresses, "There must be a mechanism to transfer the wisdom and engineering judgment of the leaders of the U.S. aerospace industry to younger professionals. A first step may be a more deliberate reaching out of the older generation to the younger and capturing their enthusiasm."

She feels this is not now happening because "our senior statesmen find the aerospace topics they're working on so compelling and urgent that they don't find the time to search out and bring along younger men and women. Younger people also need to reach out to capture the wisdom and experience of senior engineers. The age gap is easily bridged once members on both sides of the fence appreciate each other's capabilities."

SPECIALISTS AND GENERALISTS

A certain fractious adage defines a specialist and a generalist. The specialist, it allows, focuses so narrowly that eventually he or she knows everything about nothing. The generalist broadens his horizons so much, he or she eventually knows nothing about everything. There is a bit of truth in both of those comments which suggest, as my mother always used to tell me, "Do everything in moderation."

Engineers with leadership potential come in all forms, shapes and bents. They will each handle the forks in the road in different ways and with different intensities. The truly technical and narrowly focused engineer will address them in a much different way than will the more diversified generalist. The well-rounded and highly educated professional engineer will probably spend a good deal of his or her time striving to upgrade and dignify the entire profession. His or her presence will be known through efforts in general leadership in society as well as in engineering associations.

Engineers' involvement in both areas will do much to impact public policy and direction. They have much potential to help shape the future of both the engineering profession and civilization itself. The path this group of engineers takes, more than any others, will have a bigger influence in changing the public's perception of engineers as being "nerds" or "back-room types." What they do as leaders, especially if it is done with considerable passion, will be highly consequential in uplifting and enhancing our image. It will help put our profession on equal stature with the other learned professions.

What professional engineers need to be highly effective publicly is a broad perspective and education. In the future, engineering leaders who will also be society leaders must have a six- or seven-year (professional) college degree, and a life-long commitment to understanding the broader community and society at large.

Among this group will be a handful of stars like our "big-picture five." They will accomplish more — disproportionate-ly more — than any others in advancing the notion that many American engineers indeed have the right stuff to be leaders in society and the "best there ever was" when it comes to world-class engineering expertise. Hatch has such engineers in mind when he says, "We need to identify and seek out, and celebrate, those amongst us with the talent and breadth to engage in pub-lic discourse and the process." They will, indeed, need to be the true citizens of the world having the qualities to be societal leaders. They will most likely be (or already are) tomorrow's captains of industry, and our political and community leaders.

What about the rest of the field who don't end up as the superstar leaders? And what about the primarily technical engineer — the person with the four-year college degree, happy to be in the backroom (out of the limelight) doing sound engineering and computations?

For us to make a difference as a profession, we have to get out of our shells and communicate with people outside our narrow confines. And we need to speak with a unified voice on as many mutually agreed-upon issues as possible. If each of us did something — maybe wrote a short article or letter to the editor about how our expertise impacts our neighbor — much would get accomplished.

It does not matter if we have four-year technical degree or a seven-year professional degree; we are engineers. We are trained to use scientific principles and logic and be honest with our facts. We are unified in that thought process and what that implies in problem solving. All of us can afford to improve our "people" skills and commit to lifelong learning to become and stay the best in our specialty — whether as leaders or as the best narrowly focused expert in our field.

What American technical engineers of the future will face — not unlike what U.S. manufacturing workers in the recent past found out — is that others around the world will work at lower wages than we are accustomed to. Many well-qualified engineers in evolving countries work for salaries one-fourth or one-third of their U.S. counterparts.

Over the years, American engineers have maintained an edge on creativity. Our design and construction project management expertise continues to be sought after around the globe. Routine engineering tasks, on the other hand, are not the exclusive domain of Americans. Those types of engineering assignments in the future are up for grabs. They will probably go to those who do acceptable work at the lowest price.

Highly-qualified technical engineers, no matter what nationality, if they are the best — the very best — at what they do will always be in demand. So if your calling is to be a technical engineer (the expert of experts in your field), commit to an ongoing improvement program in your specialty. Many educators say today's technical knowledge becomes obsolete every seven years. So keep in mind that to get to (and stay at) the leading edge requires education long after college. And go that extra mile, by speaking out about how your engineering work fits into the "big picture" to benefit society. And support and encourage those generalists in our profession who endeavor to make it better for all of us — those dedicated to increasing the standing of engineering as a learned profession.

More and more, our young, up-and-coming engineers striving to be well-rounded professional engineers must be assisted in their efforts to position themselves for leadership roles in society. Our universities and engineering colleges must be encouraged to get serious about teaching potential engineering leaders about the importance of their work — that what they will be doing is relevant to society and life — and that they will not be making calculations, designs, drawings and specifications in a vacuum. That new treatment plant or bridge, for instance, is not just another construction project. It will change people's lives and their standards for years to come. Engineering works have a significant impact on the big picture of things.

REGISTRATION

It is embarrassing that of the 2.5 million or so engineers in the U.S., only around 10 percent are registered as professional engineers. I'm sure the medical and legal professions would never condone such statistics. Why do we engineers?

Shouldn't we as a group do something about this? Maybe change and improve the registration laws or testing requirements? Not make them less difficult, but rather make them more inclusive so that all disciplines — not just traditional civil, structural, mechanical and electrical engineers — feel they have relevancy. Or how about putting pressure on our colleges, public agencies and industry to reward those who have taken the effort to get registered as a professional?

That neither the U.S. Secretary of Transportation nor the Secretary of Energy is an engineer is, likewise, disheartening. It is akin to the U.S. Attorney General not being a lawyer or the U.S. Surgeon General not being a doctor. But even more disheartening is seeing the engineering community is not up in arms over it. It's as if we just assume that technical expertise is of no consequence in positions such as this. I wonder if the architectural community would stay silent if the architect for the Capitol were a lawyer and not an architect.

Can we not get together more often on key questions and speak to the public with a unified voice on major issues controlling and impacting our profession and industry?

TOMORROW

As engineers, we live in a time of dramatic challenges. Solving dilemmas such as global environmental and infrastructure problems will require enormous changes of both a political and technical nature. Our challenge as a profession is unmatched. If we wish, we can continue to fill purely technical roles. However, our maximum potential value to civilization's progress — and our own well-being — will not be realized unless we boldly step forward to become societal leaders and effective decision makers.

Whatever your station in life, you are part of that larger community of people called engineers. We are in this together and we can and must unify on key and basic issues. If we do, we will help make this a much better place for current and future generations.

I am reminded of a moving statement by Winston Churchill about why we are here. "What is the use of living, if not to strive for nobler causes and to make this muddled world a better place for those who will live in it after we are gone?" Engineers are truly blessed with the necessary pragmatic skills, creativity and talents to do just that — make this planet a better place, now and in the future.

BIBLIOGRAPHY

ALEXANDER, C., "One Voice," *The Institute*, July, 1997, pg 11.

AMBROSE, S., *Undaunted Courage*. New York: Simon and Schuster, 1996.

ASIMOV, I., *Asimov's New Guide To Science*. New York: Harper Collins Publishing, 1984.

AUGUSTINE, N., *Plenary Session Address - 1993 Centennial Symposium*, University of Colorado, Boulder, CO: (Printed in *CUEngineering*, No. 11, Spring 1994).

AUGUSTINE, N., "Creating a Science-Minded Workforce," *The Bridge*, Vol. 25, No. 4 (Winter 1995), pp 39-40.

BACHNER, J., *Practice Management For Design Professionals*. New York: John Wiley and Sons, Inc., 1991.

BAKER, D. and SCHAFER, T., *The Case For Public Investment*. Washington, DC: Economic Policy Institute, 1995.

BANASIAK, D. (editor), "New York tops list of states whose bridges are most in need of repair," *Roads and Bridges*, Nov., 1996, pg 18.

BARON, R. (editor), *Jefferson The Man: In His Own Words*. Golden, CO: Fulcrum/Starwood Publishing, 1993.

BENNIS, W., *On Becoming a Leader*. New York: Addison-Wesley Publishing Co., 1989.

BENNIS, W. and NANUS, B., *Leaders - The Strategies for Taking Charge*. New York: Harper & Row Publishers, 1985.

BENTON, D., *Lions Don't Need To Roar*. New York: Warner Books, 1992.

BILLINGTON, D., *The Tower and the Bridge*. New York: Basic Books, Inc., 1983.

BLACKWELL, R., *From The Edge Of The World*. Columbus: Ohio State University Press, 1995.

BORDOGNA, J., FROMM, E. and ERNST, E., "An Integrative And Holistic Engineering Education," *Journal of Science Education and Technology*, Vol. 4, No. 3, 1995.

BURNS, J. M., *Leadership*. New York: Harper and Row, 1978.

CETRON, M. and DAVIES, O., *Probable Tomorrows*. New York: St. Martin's Press, 1997.

CHAKIN, A., *A Man On The Moon*. New York: Penguin Books, 1994.

CHEN, F. and WEINGARDT, R., *Engineering Colorado*. Englewood, CO: Jacqueline Publishing, Inc., 1989.

CHENEY, M., *Tesla: Man Out of Time*. Englewood Cliffs, NJ: Prentice-Hall, 1981.

COVEY, S., *The Seven Habits of Highly Effective People*. New York: Simon and Schuster, 1989.

COX, D. and HOOVER, J., *Leadership When The Heat's On*. New York: McGraw-Hill, Inc., 1992.

COXE, W., *Marketing Architectural And Engineering Services*. New York: Van Nostrand Reinhold Co., 1971.

CRAWFORD, C., "Doctors Throw Stethoscopes Into Political Ring," *The Orlando Sentinel*, May 16, 1994, pp A1 & A5.

CRICHTON, M., *Airframe*. New York: Alfred A. Knopf, 1996.

CUSHMAN, R. (editor), *Design Professional's Handbook Of Business and Law*. New York: John Wiley and Sons, 1991.

DARLING, A., KILGOUR, F., KIRBY, R. and WITHINGTON, S., *Engineering in History*. New York: McGraw-Hill Book Co. 1956.

DRUCKER, P., *Post-Capitalist Society*. New York: Harper Collins Publishers, 1993.

DRUCKER, P., *Men, Ideas and Politics*. New York: Harper and Row, 1971.

FERRELL, R., "Get Those Electives" (Letters), *Engineering Times*, June, 1997. pg. 15.

FLORMAN, S., *The Civilized Engineer*. New York: St. Martin's Press, 1987.

FLORMAN, S., *The Introspective Engineer*. New York: St. Martin's Press, 1996.

FOX, R. L., *The Search for Alexander*. Boston: Little Brown and Company, 1980.

FULLER, B., *Ideas and Integrities*. Englewood Cliffs, NJ: Prentice-Hall, Inc., 1969.

GABLEMAN, I. (editor), *The New Engineer's Guide To Career Growth And Professional Awareness*. Piscataway, NJ: IEEE Press, 1996.

GARREAU, J., *The Nine Nations of North America*. New York: Avon Books, 1981.

GILDER, G., *Wealth and Poverty*. New York: Basic Books, 1981.

GODFREY, K., *Partnering in Design and Construction*. New York: McGraw-Hill Book Co., 1995.

GUTTMAN, H.P., *The International Consultant*. New York: McGraw-Hill, 1976.

HALEY, J., *Wooing A Harsh Mistress: Glenwood Canyon's Odyssey*. Greeley, CO: Canyon Communications, 1994.

HAMPTON, D., "Critical Issues for Engineering Managers," *ASCE Journal of Management in Engineering*, Vol. 8, No. 3, (July 1992), pp 235-246.

HARDING, F., *Rain Making*. Holbrook, MA: Adams Media Corp., 1994.

HARRISS, J., *The Tallest Tower*. Boston: Houghton Mifflin Co., 1975.

HAWKINS, S., *A Brief History Of Time*. New York: Bantam Books, 1988.

HOOVER, H., *Addresses Upon the American Road, 1950-1955*. Stanford, CA: Stanford University Press, 1955.

HOVERSTEN, P., "Day of Reckoning is Here (USA's Bridges - Middle Age Taking a Toll)," *USA Today*, August 29, 1994.

HUDSON, K., "Troubled Bridges Over Water: Maintaining the Nation's Inventory," *American City & County*, February, 1996, pp 30-47.

IACCOCA, L., *Talking Straight*. New York: Bantam Books, 1988.

JAROFF, L., "Crisis in the Labs," *Time*, Vol. 138, No. 8 (August 26, 1991), pp 44-51.

KANTER, R.M., *The Change Masters*. New York: Simon and Schuster, 1983.

KEMPER, J.D., *Engineers and Their Profession*. New York: Holt, Rinehart and Winston, 1982.

KOUZES, J. and POSNER, B., *The Leadership Challenge*. San Francisco: Jossey-Bass Publishers, 1995.

KUECKEN, J.A., *Starting and Managing Your Own Engineering Practice*. New York: Van Nostrand Reinhold, 1978.

LACOB, M., "Elevators on the Move," *Scientific American*, October 1997, pp 136-7.

LAMM, R., "Let's Build Quality Of Life," *The Denver Post*, January 11, 1998.

LATHAM, M., *Constructing The Team*. London: HMSO Publications, 1994.

LEVITT, T., *The Marketing Imagination*. New York: The Free Press, 1983.

LEWIS, B., "The Civil Engineer As Politician," *Civil Engineering*, April, 1974.

MATTINGLY, T., "A Simpler Ride Into Space," *Scientific American*, Vol. 277, No. 4, October, 1997.

MAYER, A., *The Urgent Future*, New York: McGraw-Hill Book Co., 1967.

MAXWELL, J., *Developing The Leader Within You*. Nashville, TN: Thomas Nelson Publishers, 1993.

McCULLOUGH, D., "Civil Engineers Are People," *Civil Engineering - ASCE*, Vol. 48, No. 12 (December, 1978), pp 46-50.

McCULLOUGH, D., *The Great Bridge*. New York: Simon and Schuster, 1982.

McCULLOUGH, D., *The Path Between The Seas*. New York: Simon and Schuster, 1977.

McRAE, H., *The World In 2020*. Boston: Harvard Business School Press, 1994.

MEEHAN, R., *Getting Sued and Other Tales of the Engineering Life*, Cambridge, MA: The MIT Press, 1981.

MORRIS, T., *True Success: A New Philosophy Of Excellence*. New York: Berkley Books, 1995.

MOULAKIS, A., *Beyond Utility*. Columbia, MO: University of Missouri Press, 1993.

NAISBITT, J., *Megatrends*. New York: Warner Books, 1982.

NOBLE, D. F., *America by Design*. New York: Alfred A. Knopf, 1977.

PETERSON, R., "Plotting Safe Passage To The Millennium," *Civil Engineering News*, Vol. 9, No. 8, September, 1997.

PETERS, T. and AUSTIN, N., *A Passion for Excellence - The Leadership Difference*. New York: Random House, 1985.

PETERS, T. and WATERMAN, R., Jr., *In Search of Excellence*. New York: Warner Books, 1983.

PETROSKI, H., *To Engineer is Human: The Role of Failure in Successful Design*. New York: St. Martin's Press, 1985.

POIROT, J., "Sharing The Pride," *ASCE Journal of Professional Issues*, Vol. 119, No. 3, April, 1993.

POIROT, J., "Sustainable Development," *Engineering News Record*, August 8, 1997.

PURSELL, C., Jr. (editor), *Technology in America*. Cambridge, MA: The MIT Press, 1981.

RAND, A., *Capitalism: The Unknown Ideal*. New York: Signet Books, 1967.

RIFKIN, G., "Leadership, Can It Be Learned?", *Forbes*, April 8, 1996, pp 100-112.

ROBBINS, A., *Awaken the Giant Within*. New York: Summit Books, 1991.

ROGERS, F. G., *The IBM Way*. New York: Harper and Row, 1986.

SAGAN, C., *Billions And Billions*. New York: Random House, 1997.

SANDSTROM, G., *Man the Builder*. New York: McGraw-Hill Book Co., 1970.

SCHLAGER, N. (editor), *When Technology Fails*. Detroit, MI: Gale Publishing, Inc., 1994.

SEIDEN, R. M., *Breaking Away - Engineer's Guide to a Successful Engineering Practice*. Englewood Cliffs, NJ: Prentice Hall, 1987.

SIEGEL, D., "Active PE Rolls Up Political Sleeves," *Engineering Times*, June, 1997, pg 15.

SMITH, A., *The Wealth Of Nations*. Chicago: The University of Chicago Press, 1976.

SMITH, H., *Rethinking America*. New York: Random House, 1995.

STANLEY, C. M., *The Consulting Engineer*. New York: John Wiley, 1982.

TAYLOR, J., "Warming a Chilly Classroom," *ASEE Prism*, February, 1997, pp 29-33.

THOMAS, E., *Robert E. Lee*. New York: W.W. Norton and Company, 1995.

THOMPSON, F., "Zeroing In On Critical Business Processes To Stay Ahead Of The Competition," *National Productivity Review*, Summer, 1997.

TOFFLER, A., *Future Shock*. New York: Random House, 1970.

TOWNSEND, R., *Up The Organization*. New York: Alfred A. Knopf, 1991.

WALESH, S.G., *Engineering Your Future*. Englewood Cliffs, NJ: Prentice Hall, 1995.

WEINGARDT, R.G., "Engineers and Leadership," *ASCE Journal of Professional Issues in Engineering*, Vol. 120, No. 1, (January, 1994), pp 50-57.

WEINGARDT, R.G. (editor), *Seeing Into The Future - The I-Book*, Washington, DC: America Consulting Engineers Council Publication 307, 1996.

WILL, G., "Hoover Dam: Monument to What America Once Was," *Chicago Sun-Times*, August 13, 1995.

WILSON, D.E., Jr., "Innovative Thinking is What Makes the Leaders Industry Demands," *Journal American Production and Inventory Control Society*, Vol. 7, No. 2, (1992), pp 4-5.

———— "First Consultation on Consulting Engineering Services," United Nations Industrial Development Organization (UNIDO) Report No. ID/397, September 20, 1995, Vienna, Austria.

———— "Taking Control Of Our Destiny," *PSMA Ascent*, November/December, 1995.

———— "Wary Design Firms Say No to New Work," *American Consulting Engineer*, Vol. 8, No. 1, (February 1997), pp 24-31.

National/International Engineering Conference Papers:

HOFMANN, E., "The Integration Of Environmental Considerations Into The Design Process," FIDIC Conference Paper, September, 1991, Tokyo, Japan, International Association of Consulting Engineers.

ROBERTS, D., "Engineering For Sustainable Development," AICE Conference Paper, Summer, 1993, Seattle, WA, American Institute of Chemical Engineers.

ABOUT THE AUTHOR

PROLOGUE, by Jeff Rundles

I don't really remember meeting Richard Weingardt. Some people are like that. You become friends, do projects together, talk at length about every subject from University of Colorado football (a Weingardt passion) and the aesthetics of highway bridges (another Weingardt passion), to leadership (a Weingardt crusade) and the combative nature of trial lawyers (don't get Weingardt talking), and the who, what, why, when and how the friendship ever got started fades into the unimportant mist at the edges of life.

I do know, however, that my sphere of understanding concerning the profession of engineering — and probably architecture and construction management as well — would be nothing if I hadn't met Rich Weingardt. When I was a student at the University of Michigan many years ago, I used to walk by the engineering school every day and I never even once thought that it might be interesting to find out what went on in there. What a pity. Not that I would have ended up an engineer or anything, but I certainly would have learned a lot more a lot sooner about the built-environment and the infrastructure all around me.

The fact is that I have always cared about these things, and so have so many of the people I have known in my life. We talk about whether we like buildings or not. We discuss the need for new roads and bridges, sewer systems and water treatment facilities, airports, convention centers; the list goes on and on. Trouble is, when we discuss or debate the virtues, or lack thereof, in these structures and infrastructures, we tend to focus upon the developers or politicians or civic economic booster types who drive the policies leading to construction. Until I met Rich Weingardt, I never really considered the people who would actually design or build them.

Policy making is important, of course, for it lays the groundwork for the aspirations of individuals and society and also makes the financing possible. It is, if you will, the dreaming part of the process.

But I have learned that many of these dreams take an enormous amount of imagination and skill to fulfill, and that's where the builders — the engineers and architects and constructors — come in.

As a journalist for these many years, the typical policy makers of the world have been at my doorstep or on my phone much more often than I would choose. But in the few instances that I would have a story, or an idea for a story, that might involve the special expertise of an architect or engineer, most of the time I encountered skepticism. These people were skeptical for two basic reasons, it seems to me.

First, since the "professions" have generally eschewed marketing or advertising of any type — and for a long time by direct edict of the profession's code of ethics — there seemed to be a general fear that even speaking to a member of the working press may be construed as an ethical violation.

Second, which is tied to the first since these people did not often talk to the press, they appeared to be intimidated by the press process and felt better having "no comment" policies. There are many, many people who think that the press just never gets it right. They are correct in thinking that since it would be hard for a professional journalist to get five years of engineering school and several years of experience perfect in the time it takes to do an interview.

Rather than fight through the inherent shortcomings in the press, however, architects and engineers have seemed willing to let those more adept at the process — developers, bankers, politicians and civic boosters — take all the glory and set all the policies.

Weingardt has always been the exception, and the impact he has made throughout his career is ample proof of that. Not only has he built a successful firm that has garnered a powerful reputation in engineering excellence, he has been a tireless crusader for increasing the visibility of his profession, and related professions, to business and government leaders and to the general public. He has also worked diligently in having his profession do a better job exposing its virtues to school children and college students in an almost single-handed effort to halt the decline in the number of people in this country choosing the design-build industry for a career.

He and I have forged a friendship out of a professional association that has benefited us both greatly. I have offered him the opportunity to put his views out in front of the publics reachable in the business press. He has taught me a new appreciation for the value of infrastructure — its cost factors and its impact on society — that has helped me better understand and report upon the most important business, and societal, issues of the day.

Besides, armed with the ammunition from people who actually build things has given me a better perspective concerning the pipes those civic pipe-dreamers are always talking about.

Weingardt's writings provide us with the essence of what engineering has done in the past, and what heights it can reach in the future. He is proof you don't have to go to law school to be a leader.

> — Jeff Rundles, Former Editor
> *Colorado Business Magazine* and
> *The Denver Business Journal*

BACKGROUND

Richard G. Weingardt is chairman and chief executive officer of Richard Weingardt Consultants, Inc., a consulting structural and civil engineering firm, based in Denver, CO, which he founded in 1966. He comes from a long line of builders. His father was a general contractor as was his grandfather and great-grandfather.

After graduating from the University of Colorado in 1960, he was employed as a structural engineer by the U.S. Bureau of Reclamation, Denver. Projects he worked on included dams, bridges, transmission towers and buildings such as the San Luis Generating Plant, CA, Montrose Administration Building, CO and Lewiston Dam Power Plant and Fish Hatchery, CA.

He next worked for Ketchum Konkel Ryan and Fleming, consulting engineers in Denver, on a wide range of structures. Buildings he did engineering on included Currigan Convention Center in Denver, the Antlers Hotel and Holly Sugar Office Tower, both in Colorado Springs, CO.

Since the inception of Richard Weingardt Consultants, Inc., more than 3,000 major projects worldwide — 41 states and 12 foreign countries — have been completed by his firm. RWC, Inc. has been the recipient of over 75 notable engineering excellence awards for projects such as the three concourses at the Denver International Airport, the Integrated Teaching and Learning Laboratory at the University of Colorado, Farmers Insurance Headquarters, Kansas City, MO, Jefferson County Government Center, Golden, CO and the 92nd Avenue Overpass, Westminster, CO.

Weingardt lectures internationally and is the author (or co-author) of five books and more than 300 papers on engineering, business, leadership and creativity.

For many years, he has challenged the engineering profession not only to enhance their visibility but to become citizens of the world — to take on leadership roles outside of the engineering industry. He is active in professional societies and his community. He is a past president of the American Consulting Engineers Council (ACEC), Society of Marketing Professional Services (SMPS-Colorado) and ACEC-Colorado.

Civic groups he has served on include the Colorado Historic Preservation Review Board, the state's Long-Range Planning Subcommittee and "Colorado Vision 2000." He is on the engineering advisory boards for three universities: Colorado, Texas and Denver.

The recipient of numerous professional and community awards, Weingardt was presented with the Norlin Medal in 1995 by the University of Colorado, its highest alumni recognition. In 1997, he received the Gold Medal from the Colorado Engineering Council — representing the state's 17 engineering associations — for lifetime achievement.

Weingardt is a registered professional engineer in 30 states and is a Fellow in both ACEC and the American Society of Civil Engineers.

INDEX